Impeachment
AND THE U.S. CONGRESS

March 1974

Congressional Quarterly
1414 22nd Street, N.W., Washington, D.C.

Congressional Quarterly Inc.

Congressional Quarterly Inc., an editorial research service and publishing company, serves clients in the fields of news, education, business and government. It combines specific coverage of Congress, government and politics by Congressional Quarterly with the more general subject range of an affiliated service, Editorial Research Reports.

Congressional Quarterly was founded in 1945 by Nelson and Henrietta Poynter. Its basic periodical publication was and still is the CQ *Weekly Report,* mailed to clients every Saturday. A cumulative index is published quarterly.

The CQ *Almanac,* a compendium of legislation for one session of Congress, is published every spring. *Congress and the Nation* is published every four years as a record of government for one presidential term.

Congressional Quarterly also publishes paperback books on public affairs. These include the twice-yearly *Guide to Current American Government* and such recent titles as *Watergate: Chronology of a Crisis* and *Supreme Court, Justice and the Law.*

CQ Direct Research is a consulting service which performs contract research and maintains a reference library and query desk for the convenience of clients.

Editorial Research Reports covers subjects beyond the specialized scope of Congressional Quarterly. It publishes reference material on foreign affairs, business, education, cultural affairs, national security, science and other topics of news interest. Service to clients includes a 6,000-word report four times a month bound and indexed semi-annually. Editorial Research Reports publishes paperback books in its fields of coverage. Founded in 1923, the service merged with Congressional Quarterly in 1956.

Book Service Editor: Robert A. Diamond
Major contributors: Elder Witt, Margaret Thompson.
Other contributors: Kim W. Brace, F. Rhodes Cook, Alan Ehrenhalt, Edna Frazier, Janice L. Goldstein, James W. Lawrence, Warden Moxley, Donald Smith.
Cover design: Howard Chapman. Production Supervisor: Richard C. Young. Assistant Production Supervisor: Richard Butler.

Library of Congress Cataloging in Publication Data

Congressional Quarterly, inc.
    Impeachment and the U.S. Congress
    1. Impeachments—United States. 2. United States.
Congress. House. Committee on the Judiciary.
I. Diamond, Robert A., ed. II. Title.
KF4958.C65   342'.73'062   74-5285
ISBN 0-87187-056-8

TABLE OF CONTENTS

What was the practice before this in cases where the chief Magistrate rendered himself obnoxious? Why recourse was had to assassination in wch. he was not only deprived of his life but of the opportunity of vindicating his character. It wd. be the best way therefore to provide in the Constitution for the regular punishment of the Executive when his misconduct should deserve it, and for his honorable acquittal when he should be unjustly accused.

—Benjamin Franklin, July 20, 1787
(From the Journal of James Madison, Records of the Federal Convention)

INTRODUCTION

Resolved, That the Committee on the Judiciary...is authorized and directed to investigate fully and completely whether sufficient grounds exist for the House of Representatives to exercise its constitutional power to impeach Richard M. Nixon, President of the United States of America. The committee shall report to the House of Representatives such resolutions, articles of impeachment, or other recommendations as it deems proper....

—House Resolution 803, approved Feb. 6, 1974, by a 410-4 roll-call vote.

For the first time since 1867 and for only the second time in American history, the House of Representatives in 1974 formally authorized an investigation of grounds for the impeachment of a President.

On three other occasions, Presidents have been the target of impeachment attempts. In 1843, the House rejected a resolution proposing an investigation into the possibility of impeaching John Tyler. In 1932, and again in 1933, the House rejected impeachment resolutions against Herbert Hoover. But only two Presidents—Andrew Johnson and Richard Nixon—have been the subjects of serious impeachment inquiries by House committees.

Congress has only rarely used its awesome power of impeachment against anyone. Since 1789, aside from President Andrew Johnson, only 12 other federal officials have been impeached by the House; and only four of these impeachments resulted in Senate conviction and removal from office. The four men convicted were comparatively obscure federal judges assured footnotes in history when they were found "guilty" by "two thirds of the Members present." The last House impeachment and Senate conviction occurred in 1936 when Federal Judge Halsted L. Ritter of the southern district of Florida was removed from office. Few Americans remember Judge Ritter's trial; and only five members of the current 93rd Congress (1973-74) participated in the 1936 impeachment. But events of the past 12 months have precipitated widespread interest in the subject of impeachment.

The Watergate scandal, the allegations by former White House counsel John W. Dean III of presidential involvement—and the presidential firing of Special Watergate Prosecutor Archibald Cox in October 1973—brought forth the impeachment resolutions now under investigation by the Judiciary Committee. Suddenly, impeachment no longer is considered a constitutional curiosity; the public and members of Congress are focusing their attention on impeachment and asking two questions: First, what is impeachment and how does it work? Second, should this power be exercised by Congress against President Nixon?

This book is concerned with the first of these questions. And since impeachment can not be properly understood without a close look at its history, the first two chapters provide a detailed discussion of the constitutional origins of the impeachment power, the precedents and controversial issues in past impeachments. *(p. 2-14)*. Particular attention is given to the impeachment and trial of Andrew Johnson *(p. 4)*. The chapter on precedents discusses in question and answer format those procedural issues which are likely to arise should the House and Senate proceed with impeachment; the chapter also includes the full text of the Senate rules for trial of impeachment *(p. 12)*. The full text of the articles of impeachment against Andrew Johnson and an extensive excerpt from the 1787 constitutional convention debate on impeachment appear on pages 55-59.

Beyond the historical materials, this book contains chapters placing the congressional inquiry and public debate on impeachment in the current political and legal setting. The chapter on the House Judiciary Committee examines the committee's approach to the inquiry under the leadership of Chairman Peter W. Rodino Jr. (D N.J.) and includes profiles of the committee's 38 members *(p. 15)*. Campaign contributions *(p. 26)* offer another perspective on the committee by showing which interest groups financially supported the committee members in their 1972 campaigns.

The chapters on the committee's legal staff *(p. 31)* and the President's attorneys *(p. 36)* contrast the resources of the two sides; whereas the committee has assembled a staff of 43 lawyers to conduct its inquiry, the President's legal defense staff is far smaller and the White House has had difficulties recruiting attorneys. Excerpts from documents prepared by the committee staff *(p. 33)* and by the President's staff *(p. 38)* argue for opposing definitions of what constitutes an "impeachable offense."

Two chapters of this book give useful background on the voting records of individual members of the 93rd Congress—each of whom would be called upon to vote in the event of a House impeachment and Senate trial. The presidential support voting study *(p. 42)* shows that in 1973 President Nixon received less support (on votes on which he took a position) than any President in the previous 20 years. In the chapter on group ratings *(p. 50)*, four pressure groups—liberal, conservative, labor and agricultural—select 1973 votes important to their organizations and give members of Congress a score or rating based on their support and opposition.

Robert A. Diamond
Book Service Editor
March 29, 1974

Impeachment Defined

Impeachment is the process by which the House of Representatives by majority vote formally brings charges against a federal official, thereby impeaching him. He is then tried by the Senate on those charges. If found guilty by a two-thirds vote of the senators present, the officer is removed from office and may be disqualified from holding any future federal office.

IMPEACHMENT: KEY CONGRESSIONAL POWER, RARELY USED

Impeachment is perhaps the most awesome though the least used power of Congress. In essence, it is a political action, couched in legal terminology, directed against a ranking official of the federal government. The House of Representatives is the prosecutor. The Senate chamber is the courtroom; and the Senate is the judge and jury. The final penalty is removal from office and possible disqualification from further office. There is no appeal.

Thirteen officers have been impeached by the House since 1789: one President, one cabinet officer, one senator and 10 federal judges. Of these 13, 12 cases reached the Senate. Of the 12 cases reaching the Senate, two were dismissed, six resulted in acquittal and four ended in conviction. *(p. 8)*

All of the convictions involved federal judges: John Pickering of the district court for New Hampshire, in 1804; West H. Humphreys of the eastern, middle and western districts of Tennessee in 1862; Robert W. Archbald of the Commerce Court, in 1913; and Halsted L. Ritter of the southern district of Florida, in 1936.

Two of the impeachments traditionally have stood out from all the rest. They involved Justice Samuel Chase of the Supreme Court in 1805 and President Andrew Johnson in 1868, the two most powerful and important federal officials ever subjected to the process. Both were impeached by the House—Chase for partisan conduct on the bench; Johnson for violating the Tenure of Office Act—and both were acquitted by the Senate after sensational trials. Behind both impeachments lay intensely partisan politics. Chase, a Federalist, was a victim of attacks on the Supreme Court by Jeffersonian Democrats, who had planned to impeach Chief Justice John Marshall if Chase was convicted. President Johnson was a victim of Radical Republicans opposed to his reconstruction policies after the Civil War. *(p. 4)*

Purpose of Impeachment

Based on specific constitutional authority, the impeachment process was designed "as a method of national inquest into the conduct of public men," according to Alexander Hamilton in Federalist No. 65. The Constitution declares that impeachment proceedings may be brought against "the President, Vice President and all civil officers of the United States," without explaining who is, or is not, a "civil officer." In practice, however, the overwhelming majority of impeachment proceedings have been directed against federal judges, who hold lifetime appointments "during good behavior," and cannot be removed by any other method. Nine of the 12 impeachment cases that have reached the Senate have involved federal judges. Federal judges also have figured prominently in the numerous resolutions and investigations in the House that have failed to result in impeachment.

Others whose impeachment has been sought include cabinet members, diplomats, customs collectors, a senator and a U.S. district attorney. These officials are subject to removal by dismissal or explusion as well as by impeachment, and it seldom has been necessary to resort to full-scale impeachment proceedings to bring about their removal. Proceedings against the only senator to be impeached, William Blount of Tennessee, were dismissed in 1799 after Blount had been expelled from the Senate in 1797. War Secretary William W. Belknap, the only Cabinet member to be tried by the Senate, was acquitted in 1876 largely because senators questioned their authority to try Belknap, who had resigned as secretary several months before the trial.

The House Judiciary Committee twice has ruled that certain federal officials were not subject to impeachment. In 1833, the committee determined that a territorial judge was not a civil officer within the meaning of the Constitution because he held office for only four years and could be removed at any time by the President. In 1926, the committee said that a commissioner of the District of Columbia was immune from impeachment be-

---

Constitution on Impeachment

Article I, Section 2. "The House of Representatives...shall have the sole Power of Impeachment."

Article I, Section 3. "The Senate shall have the sole Power to try all Impeachments. When sitting for that Purpose, they shall be on Oath of Affirmation. When the President of the United States is tried, the Chief Justice shall preside: And no Person shall be convicted without the Concurrence of two thirds of the Members present.

"Judgment in Cases of Impeachment shall not extend further than to removal from Office and disqualification to hold and enjoy any Office of Honor, Trust or Profit under the United States: but the Party convicted shall nevertheless be liable and subject to Indictment, Trial, Judgment and Punishment, according to Law."

Article II, Section 2. The President "shall have Power to grant Reprieves and Pardons for Offenses against the United States, except in Cases of Impeachment."

Article II, Section 4. "The President, Vice President and all civil Officers of the United States shall be removed from Office on Impeachment for, and Conviction, of, Treason, Bribery, or other high Crimes and Misdemeanors."

Article III, Section 2. "The Trial of all Crimes, except in Cases of Impeachment, shall be by jury...."

cause he was an officer of the District and not a civil officer of the United States.

History: Curbing the Executive

Impeachment as a constitutional process dates from 14th century England when the fledgling Parliament sought to make the King's advisers accountable. The monarch, who was considered incapable of wrongdoing, was immune. Impeachment was used against ministers and judges whom the legislature believed guilty of breaking the law or carrying out the unpopular orders of the king. The system was based on the common law and the House of Lords could inflict the death penalty on those it found guilty.

Grounds for impeachment included both criminal and non-criminal activity. Joseph Story, in his *Commentaries on the Constitution of the United States* (1905), wrote: "Lord chancellors and judges and other magistrates have not only been impeached for bribery and acting grossly contrary to the duties of their office, but for misleading their sovereign by unconstitutional opinions and for attempts to subvert the fundamental laws and introduce arbitrary power."

In the mid 15th century, after the conviction of the Duke of Suffolk, impeachment fell into disuse. This was in large measure due to the ability of the Tudor Monarchs to force Parliament to remove unwanted officials by bills of attainder or pains and penalties. In the early 17th century, the excesses and absolutist tendencies of the Stuart kings prompted Parliament to revive its impeachment power to curb the monarch by removing his favorite aides.

The struggle between the king and the Commons came to a head with the impeachment of Charles the First's minister, the Earl of Strafford, in 1642. The Earl was impeached by the House of Commons for subverting the fundamental law and introducing an arbitrary and tyrannical government. While the charge was changed to a bill of attainder in the House of Lords, Raoul Berger writes that "his impeachment may be regarded as the opening gun in the struggle whereby the Long Parliament prevented the English monarchy from hardening into an absolutism of the type then becoming general in Europe."

More than 50 impeachments were brought to the House of Lords for trial between 1620 and 1787 when the American constitution was being written. As the Framers toiled in Philadelphia, the long impeachment and trial of Warren Hastings was in progress in London. Hastings was charged with oppression, cruelty, bribery and fraud as colonial administrator and first governor general in India. The trial before the House of Lords lasted from Feb. 13, 1788 to April 23, 1795. Hastings was acquitted, but by that time, impeachment was widely regarded as unnecessary—because of ministerial responsibility to parliament—and overly cumbersome. The last impeachment trial in Britain occurred in 1806.

Constitutional Convention

In America, colonial governments and early state constitutions followed the British pattern of trial on impeachment before the upper legislative body on charges brought by the lower house.

Despite these precedents, a major controversy arose over the impeachment process in the Constitutional Convention. The issue was whether the Senate should try impeachments. Opposing that role for the Senate, Madison and Pinckney asserted that it would make the President too dependent on the legislative branch. Suggested alternative trial bodies included the "national judiciary," the Supreme Court or the assembled chief justices of state supreme courts. It was argued, however, that such bodies would be too small and perhaps even susceptible to corruption. In the end, the Senate was agreed to. Hamilton (a Senate opponent during the Convention) asked later in the Federalist: "Where else than in the Senate could have been found a tribunal sufficiently dignified, or sufficiently independent?"

Impeachable Crimes. A lesser issue was the definition of impeachable crimes. In the original proposals, the President was to be removed on impeachment and conviction "for mal or corrupt conduct," or for "malpractice or neglect of duty." Later, the wording was changed to "treason, bribery or corruption," and then to "treason and bribery" alone. Contending that "treason and bribery" were too narrow, George Mason proposed adding "mal-administration," but switched to "other high crimes and misdemeanors against the state" when Madison said that "mal-administration" was too broad. A final revision made impeachable crimes "treason, bribery or other high crimes and misdemeanors."

The provisions of the Constitution on impeachment were scattered through the first three articles. To the House was given the "sole power of impeachment." The Senate was given "the sole power to try all impeachments." Impeachments could be brought against "the President, Vice President, and all civil officers of the United States" for "treason, bribery or other high crimes or misdemeanors." Conviction meant "removal from office and disqualification to hold" further public office.

The first attempt to use the impeachment power was made in 1796. A petition from residents of the Northwest Territory, submitted to the House on April 25, accused Judge George Turner of the territorial supreme court of arbitrary conduct. The petition was referred briefly to a special House committee and then was referred to Attorney General Charles Lee. Impeachment proceedings were dropped after Lee said, May 9, that the territorial government would prosecute Turner in the territorial courts.

Procedures in Impeachment

The first impeachment proceedings, against Turner, failed to provide precedents for later impeachments. In fact, the process has been used so infrequently and under such widely varying circumstances that no uniform practice has emerged.

At various times impeachment proceedings have been initiated by the introduction of a resolution by a member, by a letter or message from the President, by a grand jury action forwarded to the House from a territorial legislature, by a memorandum setting forth charges, by a resolution authorizing a general investigation, or by a resolution reported by the House Judiciary Committee. The five cases to reach the Senate since 1900 were based on Judiciary Committee resolutions.

After submission of the charges, a committee investigation has been undertaken. If the charges have been

(Continued on p. 6)

President Andrew Johnson's Impeachment in 1868: . . .

Impeachment is the ultimate limitation on the power of the President. The only presidential impeachment occurred in 1868. President Andrew Johnson was charged with violation of a federal statute, the Tenure of Office Act. But in addition, the procedure was a profoundly political struggle between irreconcilable forces.

Questions such as control of the Republican Party, how to deal with the South in a state of chaos following the Civil War, and monetary and economic policy all had an effect on the process.

Johnson as President was an anomaly. Lincoln's running mate in 1864, he was a southerner at a time when the South was out of the union; a Jacksonian Democrat who believed in states' rights, hard money, and minimal federal government activity running with an administration pursuing a policy of expansion both in the money supply and the role of government; a man who had little regard for the Negro in the midst of a party many of whose members were actively seeking to guarantee the rights of the newly freed slaves.

In these contradictions lay the basis for an inevitable conflict. The interplay of personalities and policies decreed that the conflict would result in an impeachment process.

Johnson had been the only member of the U.S. Senate from a seceding southern state (Tennessee) to remain loyal to the Union in 1861. Lincoln later made him military governor of Tennessee and chose him as his running mate in 1864 as a southerner and Democrat who was also a loyalist and in favor of prosecuting the war.

Sources

Michael Les Benedict, *The Impeachment and Trial of Andrew Johnson,* W. W. Norton and Company Inc., New York, 1973.

Raoul Berger, *Impeachment: The Constitutional Problems,* Harvard University Press, Cambridge, 1973.

James G. Blaine, *Twenty Years of Congress, 1861-1881,* The Henry Hill Publishing Company, Norwich, Conn., 1886.

On Lincoln's death in 1865, this outsider without allies or connections in the Republican Party succeeded to the presidency. Johnson's ideas on what should have been done to reconstruct and readmit the southern states to representation clashed with the wishes of a majority of Congress, overwhelmingly controlled by the Republicans.

Among the latter, there was a strong desire to secure the Negroes in their rights. Some had selfish motives: black votes and support were necessary for the Republicans to maintain their political hegemony. Others were more idealistic: the ex-slaves were helpless and had to be protected by the federal government, or they would quickly lose their new freedom.

Congress was divided into roughly three groups. The small minority of Democrats supported the President. About half the Republicans were known as "radicals," because they favored strong action to revolutionize southern society, by harsh military means if necessary. The other half of the Republicans were more conservative; while unwilling to go as far as the radicals, they wanted to make sure the South did not return to the unquestioned control of those who ruled it before the Civil War.

Over the years 1866-69, the conservative Republicans were repeatedly thrown into coalition with the radicals, often against their wishes. The radicals always counted on Johnson to help them out by behaving aggressively and uncompromisingly. They were usually confirmed in their expectations.

Upon taking office, Johnson began to pursue Lincoln's mild and tolerant reconstruction plans. The new President felt that a few basics were all that needed to be secured: abolition of slavery; ratification of the 13th Amendment, which abolished slavery in all states; repudiation of all state debts contracted by the Confederate governments; nullification of secession. When the southern states had done these things, Johnson felt they should be readmitted.

But Republicans wanted more: a Freedmen's Bureau, to protect and provide services for the ex-slaves, a civil rights bill guaranteeing the Negroes their rights, and an over-all plan of reconstruction providing for temporary military governments in the South.

Throughout 1866, Johnson and Congress battled over these issues. In February, the President vetoed the Freedmen's Bureau bill. The Senate failed to override, but this was the last Johnson veto to be sustained. For the rest of the year, bill after bill was passed over Johnson's veto, including a second Freedmen's Bureau bill, a civil rights bill and, in early 1867, a reconstruction bill and the Tenure of Office Act.

The Tenure of Office Act, the violation of which was to be the legal basis for Johnson's impeachment, was passed over his veto March 2, 1867. The act forbade the President to remove civil officers (appointed with the consent of the Senate) without the approval of the Senate. Its purpose was to protect incumbent Republican officeholders from executive retaliation if they did not support the President. Johnson had made wholesale removals from rank-and-file federal offices both during and after the election campaign of 1866.

UNSUCCESSFUL ASHLEY RESOLUTION

About the time the Tenure of Office Act was being debated, the first moves toward impeachment began. On Jan. 7, 1867, two Missouri representatives, Benjamin F. Loan (R Mo. 1863-69) and John R. Kelso (R Mo. 1865-67), attempted in turn to introduce resolutions in the House proposing impeachment, but each was prevented by parliamentary maneuver.

But later the same day, Rep. James M. Ashley (R Ohio 1859-69) rose on a question of privilege and formally charged the President with high crimes and misdemeanors. (Ashley was the great-grandfather of Rep. Thomas L. Ashley (D Ohio), who was elected in 1954 in the same district as his ancestor.)

... An Inevitable Clash with an Unpopular President

Ashley made general charges, and no specific violations of law were mentioned. Most members recognized the charges as basically political grievances rather than illegal acts. The matter was referred to the House Judiciary Committee, which reported on March 2, 1867, two days before the expiration of the 39th Congress, that the committee had reached no conclusion. Its members recommended that the matter be given further study by the next Congress.

On March 7, 1867, the third day of the 40th Congress, Ashley again introduced his resolution, and it was referred to the Judiciary Committee for further investigation. The committee studied the matter throughout the year and issued a report on Nov. 25, 1867. A majority of the committee reported an impeachment resolution. When the House voted on the matter on Dec. 7, the radicals suffered a crushing defeat. The resolution calling for impeachment was turned down, 57 to 108.

SUCCESSFUL SECOND TRY

Johnson appeared to have won. But, observed James G. Blaine in his memoirs, "Those best acquainted with the earnestness of purpose and the determination of the leading men who had persuaded themselves that the safety of the Republic depended upon the destruction of Johnson's official power, knew that the closest watch would be kept upon every action of the President, and if an apparently justifying cause could be found the project of his removal would be vigorously renewed." Within a month, the radicals found their issue.

Johnson had long wanted to rid himself of Secretary of War Edwin M. Stanton. Stanton was a close ally of the radical Republicans. After repeatedly trying to get him to resign, Johnson suspended him on Dec. 12, 1867. On Jan. 13, 1868, the Senate refused to concur, thus, under the terms of the Tenure of Office Act, reinstating Stanton.

Apparently flushed by his recent victory on the impeachment issue in the House, Johnson decided to force the issue. He dismissed Stanton on Feb. 21, citing the power and authority vested in him by the Constitution. In effect, he was declaring the Tenure of Office Act unconstitutional and refusing to abide by it.

This action enraged Congress, driving conservative Republicans into alliance with the radicals on impeachment. A House resolution on impeachment was immediately offered and was referred to the Committee on Reconstruction, headed by Rep. Thaddeus Stevens (R Pa. 1859-68; Whig 1849-53), one of the radical Republican leaders. The next day, Feb. 22, the committee reported a resolution favoring impeachment. The House vote, taken two days later, was 126 to 47 in favor, on a strict party-line basis.

TRIAL IN THE SENATE

The House took the next step of drawing up the specific articles of impeachment and appointing managers to present and argue the charges before the Senate. There were 11 articles in all, the main one concerning Johnson's removal of Stanton in contravention of the Tenure of Office Act.

Between the time of the House action and the beginning of the trial in the Senate, the conservative Republicans had time to reflect. One of the main objects of their reflection was fiery Ben Wade of Ohio. Wade was president pro tem of the Senate and, under the succession law then in effect, was next in line for the presidency. He was also one of the most radical of the radical Republicans, a hard-liner on southern reconstruction and a monetary expansionist—anathema to conservatives.

Another concern of both factions of Republicans was the upcoming national convention and presidential election. Conservatives were in favor of nominating Gen. Ulysses S. Grant, a hero in the North after the Civil War. They viewed him as the most likely candidate to win and were confident they could control him and keep him from adopting radical policies. Radicals were anxious to gain control of the presidency to prevent Grant's nomination and dictate the party's platform.

The trial started March 30, when one of the House managers made the opening argument. Although other charges were presented against the President, the House managers relied mainly on Johnson's removal of Stanton as a direct violation of the Tenure of Office Act. One of the House managers revealed the bitter emotions prevailing at the time when he said, "The world in after times will read the history of the administration of Andrew Johnson as an illustration of the depth to which political and official perfidy can descend."

By May 11, the Senate was ready to ballot. The first vote was taken May 16th on the 11th article, which was a summary of many of the charges set forth in some of the preceding articles. The result was 35 guilty, 19 not guilty. If one vote had switched, the necessary two-thirds would have been reached. Seven Republican senators joined the 12 Democrats in supporting the President.

After the first vote, the Senate adjourned as a court of impeachment until May 26. When they reconvened on that date, two more ballots were taken, on the second and third articles of impeachment. The results were the same as on the first ballot, 35 to 19. The Senate then abandoned the remaining articles and adjourned as a court of impeachment.

UNCONSTITUTIONAL GROUNDS

The Tenure of Office Act was virtually repealed early in Grant's administration, once the Republicans had control of the appointing power, and was entirely repealed in 1887. And in 1926, the Supreme Court declared, "The power to remove...executive officers... is an incident of the power to appoint them, and is in its nature an executive power." (*Myers vs. United States*) The opinion, written by Chief Justice William Howard Taft, himself a former president, referred to the Tenure of Office Act and declared that it had been unconstitutional.

(Continued from p. 3)

supported by the investigation, the committee has reported an impeachment resolution, which in four of the five post-1900 cases has included articles of impeachment. The impeachment resolution has been subject to adoption by majority vote. In earlier cases, the impeachment articles were drafted by a select committee named by the House Speaker or by simple resolution. Like the impeachment resolution, the articles too have been subject to adoption by majority vote.

The next step, after the House has adopted an impeachment resolution and articles of impeachment, has been selection of House managers to direct the proceedings in the Senate. House managers have been chosen by a resolution fixing the number of managers and authorizing the Speaker to appoint them, by a resolution fixing the number and making the appointments, and by ballot, with a majority vote for each candidate. Once selected, the House managers have appeared at the bar of the Senate to inform the upper house of the impending impeachment trial and to present the articles of impeachment. The Senate, in turn, has informed the House when it is ready to proceed.

The full House may attend the trial, but the House managers have been its representatives at the proceedings. Following Senate rules adopted March 2, 1868, the trial has been conducted in a fashion similar to a court trial for a criminal offense. Both sides may present witnesses and evidence, and the defendant has been allowed counsel and the right of cross-examination. If the President is on trial, the Constitution requires the Chief Justice of the Supreme Court to preside. The Constitution is silent on a presiding officer for lesser defendants, but Senate practice has been for the Vice President or the President pro tempore to preside. Procedural questions during trial have been decided by majority vote, but conviction has required, according to the Constitution, approval of two-thirds of the Senators present. A separate vote on each article is required by Senate rules, and a two-thirds vote on a single article is sufficient for conviction. Removal upon conviction is required by the Constitution, although the Senate at times has voted removal after conviction. Disqualification is not mandatory; only two of the four convictions have been accompanied by disqualification, which has been subject to a majority vote.

Controversial Questions

Three major issues have dominated the history of the impeachment power: the definition of impeachable offenses, possible senatorial conflicts of interest and alternative removal methods for federal judges.

Impeachable Offenses. "Treason" and "bribery," as constitutionally designated impeachable crimes, have raised little debate, for treason is defined elsewhere in the Constitution and bribery is a well-defined act. "High crimes and misdemeanors," however, have been anything that the prosecution has wanted to make them. An endless debate has surrounded the phrase, pitting broad constructionists, who have viewed impeachment as a political weapon, against narrow constructionists, who have regarded impeachment as being limited to offenses indictable at common law.

The constitutional debates seemed to indicate that impeachment was to be regarded as a political weapon. Narrow constructionists quickly won a major victory,

---

Johnson Impeachment Votes

The Senate voted on only three of the 11 articles of impeachment against President Andrew Johnson. The President was acquitted on each article by identical votes of 35-19, with 36 "guiltys" necessary for conviction. The roll call on the three votes follows *(Johnson impeachment p. 4):*

Guilty: Anthony (R R.I.), Cameron (R Pa.), Cattel (R N.J.), Chandler (R Mich.), Cole (R Calif.), Conkling (Union Republican N.Y.), Conness (Union Republican Calif.), Corbett (Union Republican Ore.), Cragin (American N.H.), Drake (R Mo.), Edmunds (R Vt.), Ferry (R Conn.), Frelinghuysen (R N.J.), Harlan (R Iowa), Howard (R Mich.), Howe (Union Republican Wis.), Morgan (Union Republican N.Y.), Morrill (R Maine), Morrill (Union Republican Vt.), Morton (Union Republican Ind.), Nye (R Nev.), Patterson (R N.H.), Pomeroy (R Kan.), Ramsey (R Minn.), Sherman (R Ohio), Sprague (R R.I.), Stewart (R Nev.), Sumner (R Mass.), Thayer (R Neb.), Tipton (R Neb.), Wade (R Ohio), Willey (R W. Va.), Williams (Union Republican Ore.), Wilson (R Mass.), Yates (Union Republican Ill.).

Not guilty: Bayard (D Del.), Buckalew (D Pa.), Davis (D Ky.), Dixon (R Conn.), Doolittle (R Wis.), Fessenden (R Maine), Fowler (Union Republican Tenn.), Grimes (R Iowa), Henderson (D Mo.), Hendricks (D Ind.), Johnson (D Md.), McCreery (D Ky.), Norton (Union Conservative Minn.), Patterson (D Tenn.), Ross (R Kan.), Saulsbury (D Del.), Trumbull (R Ill.), Van Winkle (Unionist W. Va.), Vickers (D Md.).

---

though, when Chase was acquitted, using as a defense the argument that he had committed no indictable offense. The narrow constructionists continued to prevail when President Johnson also was acquitted on a similar defense. His lawyers argued that conviction could result only from commission of high criminal offenses against the United States.

The only two convictions to date in the 20th century suggest that the broad constructionists still have powerful arguments. The 20th century convictions removed Robert W. Archbald, associate judge of the U.S. Commerce Court, in 1913, and Halsted L. Ritter, U.S. judge for the southern district of Florida, in 1936. Archbald was convicted of soliciting for himself and for friends valuable favors from railroad companies, some of which were litigants in his court. It was conceded, however, that he had committed no indictable offense. Ritter was convicted for conduct in a receivership case which raised serious doubts about his integrity.

Ritter's was the last impeachment to reach the Senate. But the debate over impeachable offenses is certain to be revived in future Senate cases.

Raoul Berger, author of the much-praised *Impeachment: The Constitutional Problem* (1973), believes that the grounds for removal lie somewhere between the English jurist Sir William Blackstone's assertion that an impeachment "is a prosecution of the already known and established law" and Rep. Gerald R. Ford (R Mich.) who, in proposing the impeachment of Supreme Court

Justice William O. Douglas on April 15, 1970, declared: "An impeachable offense is whatever a majority of the House of Representatives considers it to be at a given moment in history; conviction results from whatever offense or offenses two-thirds of the other body considers to be sufficiently serious to require removal of the accused from office."

Conflicts of Interest. An equally controversial issue, particularly in earlier impeachment trials, concerned the partisan political interests of senators, which raised serious doubt about their impartiality as jurors.

President Johnson's potential successor, for example, was the president pro tempore of the Senate, since there was a vacancy in the vice presidency. Sen. Benjamin F. Wade (R Ohio), president pro tempore, took part in the trial and voted—for conviction. On the other hand, Andrew Johnson's son-in-law, Sen. David T. Patterson (D Tenn.), also took part in the trial and voted—for acquittal.

In the Johnson trial and in others, senators have been outspoken critics or supporters of the defendant, yet have participated in the trial and have voted on the articles. Some senators who had held seats in the House when the articles of impeachment first came up, and had voted on them there, have failed to disqualify themselves during the trial. On occasion, intense outside lobbying for, and against, the defendant has been aimed at senators. Senators have testified as witnesses at some trials and then voted on the articles.

Senators may request to be excused from the trial, and in recent cases senators have disqualified themselves when possible conflicts of interest arose.

Removal of Judges. Two forces have combined in the continuing search for an alternative method of removal for federal judges. One force has been led by members of Congress anxious to free the Senate, faced by an enormous legislative workload, from the time-consuming process of sitting as a court of impeachment. The other force has been led by members anxious to restrict judicial power by providing a simpler and swifter means of removal than the cumbersome and unwieldy impeachment process.

The search to date has been unsuccessful. Efforts to revise and accelerate the impeachment process have failed. So, too, have attempts to amend the Constitution to limit the tenure of federal judges to a definite term of years. A more recent approach has been to seek legislation providing for a judicial trial and judgment of removal for federal judges violating "good-behavior" standards. The House passed such a bill on Oct. 22, 1941, by a 124-122 vote, but it died in the Senate.

A 1947 report by the Legislative Reference Service of the Library of Congress concluded:

"1. There is no power in the Executive or Legislative Branches of the Government to remove or limit the tenure of Supreme Court justices, or, indeed, any judges of constitutional courts, except as Congress is expressly authorized to act by impeachment for lack of good behavior....

"2. Means of removal other than impeachment and limitations on tenure could be provided for by constitutional amendment. Among such methods of removal could be that of legislative address.

"3. Congress perhaps can constitutionally provide for judicial removal of Federal judges for lack of good behavior....While the good behavior tenure clause never has been construed by the Supreme Court, it has been contended that the clause must be read with a view to changing needs, and that Congress, therefore, might define the term so as to allow judicial removal for any form of conduct or neglect which according to modern notions tends to corruption or inefficiency."

Attempted Impeachments

Many proposed impeachments have failed to come to a vote in the House because the defendant died or because he resigned or received another appointment, removing him from the disputed office. Among the unsuccessful impeachment attempts have been moves against two Presidents, a vice president, two cabinet officers, and a Supreme Court justice.

Tyler. The House on Jan. 10, 1843, rejected by an 84-127 vote a resolution by Rep. John M. Botts to investigate the possibility of initiating impeachment proceedings against President Tyler. Tyler had become a political outcast, ostracized by both Democrats and Whigs, but impeachment apparently was too strong a measure to take against him.

Colfax. A move developed in 1873 to impeach Vice President Schuyler Colfax because of his involvement in the Credit Mobilier scandal. The matter was dropped when the Judiciary Committee recommended against impeachment on the ground that Colfax had purchased his Credit Mobilier stock before coming Vice President.

Daugherty. A similar move to impeach Attorney General Harry M. Daugherty in 1922 on account of his action, or lack of action, in the Teapot Dome affair was dropped in 1923 when a congressional investigation of the scandal got under way. Daugherty was forced by President Coolidge to tender his resignation, March 28, 1924.

Mellon. A running fight between Rep. Wright Patman (D Texas) and Secretary of the Treasury Andrew W. Mellon over Federal economic policy in the depression came to a head in 1932. Patman on Jan. 6 demanded Mellon's impeachment on the ground of conflicting financial interests. To put an end to that move, President Hoover on Feb. 5 nominated Mellon to be ambassador to Great Britain and the Senate confirmed the nomination the same day. Mellon resigned his Treasury post a week later to take on his new duties.

Hoover. Two depression-era attempts by Rep. Louis T. McFadden (R Pa.) to impeach President Hoover on general charges of usurping legislative powers and violating constitutional and statutory law were rejected by the House. The first attempt was tabled Dec. 13, 1932, by a 361-8 vote; the second attempt was tabled Jan. 17, 1933, by a 344-11 vote.

Douglas. Associate Justice William O. Douglas of the Supreme Court has been subjected to several impeachment attempts. In 1970, two resolutions for Douglas's impeachment were introduced in the midst of a bitter conflict between President Nixon and the Senate over Senate rejection of two Supreme Court nominations. Among the charges cited were possible financial conflicts similar to those that had led to Senate rejection of the Nixon nominees for the Court. A special House Judiciary Subcommittee on Dec. 3 voted 3-1 that no grounds existed for impeachment.

THIRTEEN IMPEACHMENTS RESULTED IN FOUR CONVICTIONS

(See page 11 for Congressional Votes)

1. Name: William Blount (1797-99). **Position:** Senator. **Charge.** Attempt to keep an Indian agent from performing duty. **Decision.** Senate dismissed impeachment proceedings after voting to expel Blount.

On July 3, 1797, President John Adams sent to the House and Senate a letter from Sen. William Blount (Tenn.) to James Carey, a U.S. interpreter to the Cherokee Nation of Indians. The letter told of Blount's plans to launch an attack by Indians and frontiersmen, aided by a British fleet, against Louisiana and Spanish Florida to achieve their transfer to British control. Adams' action initiated the first proceedings to result in impeachment by the House and consideration by the Senate.

In the Senate, Blount's letter was referred to a select committee, which recommended his expulsion for "a high misdemeanor, entirely inconsistent with his public trust and duty as a Senator." The Senate expelled Blount on July 8 by a 25-1 vote.

The House, meanwhile, July 7 adopted a committee resolution impeaching Blount, and on the same day it appointed a committee to prepare articles of impeachment. On Jan. 29, 1798, the House adopted five articles accusing Blount of attempting to influence the Indians for the benefit of the British.

Senate proceedings did not begin until Dec. 17, 1798. Blount challenged the proceedings, contending that they violated his right to a trial by jury, that he was not a civil officer within the meaning of the Constitution, that he was not charged with a crime committed while a civil officer, and that courts of common law were competent to try him on the charges. On Jan. 11, 1799, the Senate by a 14-11 vote dismissed the charges for lack of jurisdiction. Citing the Senate vote, Vice President Thomas Jefferson ruled Jan. 14, that the Senate was without jurisdiction in the case, thus ending the proceedings.

2. Name. John Pickering (1803-4). **Position.** Federal judge. **Charge.** Misconduct in a trial and being intoxicated. **Decision.** Removal from office.

In a partisan move to oust a Federalist judge, President Jefferson on Feb. 4, 1803, sent a complaint to the House citing John Pickering, U.S. judge for the district of New Hampshire. The complaint was referred to a special committee, and on March 2 the House adopted a committee resolution impeaching the judge. A committee was appointed Oct. 20 to prepare articles of impeachment, and the House on Dec. 30 by voice vote agreed to four articles charging Pickering with irregular judicial procedures, loose morals and drunkenness. The judge, who was known to be insane at the time, did not attend the Senate trial, which began March 8, 1804, and ended March 12, with votes of 19-7 for conviction on each of the four articles. The Senate then voted 20-6 to remove Pickering from office, but it declined to consider disqualifying him from further office.

3. Name. Samuel Chase (1804-1805). **Position.** Associate Justice of the Supreme Court. **Charge.** Misconduct in trials impairing the court's respect. **Decision.** Acquitted.

In an equally partisan attack on another Federalist judge, the House on Jan. 7, 1804, by an 81-40 vote adopted a resolution for an investigation of Chase and of Richard Peters, a U.S. district court judge in Pennsylvania. Ostensibly, the investigation was to study their conduct during a recent treason trial. The House dropped further action against Peters by voice vote on March 12. On the same day, by a 72-32 vote, it adopted a committee resolution to impeach Chase. A committee was appointed to draw up articles, and the House in a series of votes on Dec. 4, 1804, agreed to the eight articles, charging Chase with harsh and partisan conduct on the bench and with unfairness to litigants.

The trial began Feb. 9, 1805; Chase appeared in person. The Senate voting on March 1 failed to produce the two-thirds majority required for conviction on any of the eight articles; "not-guilty" votes outnumbered the "guilty" votes on five of the articles.

4. Name. James H. Peck (1830-1831). **Position.** Federal judge. **Charge.** Misconduct in office by misuse of contempt power. **Decision.** Acquitted.

On Jan. 7, 1830, the House adopted a resolution authorizing an investigation of Peck's conduct. On April 24, the House by a 123-49 vote adopted a Judiciary Committee resolution impeaching Peck, and later the same day it appointed a committee to prepare articles of impeachment. A single article was adopted May 1 by voice vote charging Peck with setting an unreasonable and oppressive penalty for contempt of court. The trial stretched from Dec. 20, 1830, to Jan. 31, 1831, when 21 senators voted for conviction and 22 for acquittal.

√ **5. Name.** West H. Humphreys (1862). **Position.** Federal judge. **Charge.** Supported secession and held Confederate office. **Decision.** Removed from office.

During the Civil War, Humphreys, a U.S. judge for the east, middle and west districts of Tennessee, accepted an appointment as a Confederate judge, without resigning from his Union judicial assignment. Aware of the situation the House on Jan. 8, 1862, by voice vote adopted a resolution authorizing an inquiry. On May 6, the House, also by voice vote, adopted a Judiciary Committee resolution impeaching Humphreys. On May 19, seven articles of impeachment were adopted. Humphreys could not be personally served with the impeachment summons because he had fled Union territory. He neither appeared at the trial nor contested the charges. In a one-day trial June 26, the Senate convicted Humphreys on all except one charge, removed him from office by a 38-0 vote and disqualified him from further office on a 36-0 vote.

6. Name. Andrew Johnson (1867-1868). **Position.** President of the United States. **Charge.** That he removed Secretary of War contrary to an act of Congress and criticized Congress. **Decision.** Acquitted.

> **Sources.** *The Congressional Globe; Congressional Record;* House Judiciary Committee. *Impeachment: Selected Materials,* October, 1973; *Impeachment: Selected Materials on Procedure,* January 1974; *Constitutional Grounds for Presidential Impeachment* February, 1974.

The House adopted a resolution in 1867 authorizing the Judiciary Committee to inquire into the conduct of President Johnson. A majority of the committee recommended impeachment, but the House voted against the resolution 57-108. In 1868, however, the House authorized an inquiry by the Committee on Reconstruction, which reported an impeachment resolution after President Johnson had removed Secretary of War Stanton from office. The House Feb. 24 voted to impeach Johnson, 126-47.

Nine of the 11 articles drawn by a select committee and adopted by the House related solely to the President's removal of Stanton; articles 10 and 11 were broader in scope. The Senate voted only on three of the articles, and Johnson was acquitted on each, 35 "guilty" to 19 "not guilty," one vote short of the two-thirds required to convict. *(Details p. 4)*

7. Name. Mark H. Delahay (1873). **Position.** Federal judge. **Charge.** Misconduct in office, unsuitable personal habits, including intoxication. **Decision.** Resigned before articles of impeachment prepared, hence no Senate action.

In 1872 the House adopted a resolution authorizing an investigation of district judge Delahay. The Judiciary Committee in 1873 proposed a resolution of impeachment, which the House adopted. Delahay resigned before the articles of impeachment were prepared, and the matter was not pursued further by the House.

8. Name. William W. Belknap (1876). **Position.** Secretary of War (resigned). **Charge.** That he received money for appointing and continuing in office a post trader at Ft. Sill, Okla. **Decision.** Acquitted.

Faced with widespread corruption and incompetence among high officers of the Grant administration, the House in 1876 initiated a number of inquiries, resulting in adoption March 2 of a resolution of impeachment. Despite the fact that Belknap had resigned, the Judiciary Committee continued work on impeachment articles, and the House April 3 agreed to five articles of impeachment.

As pre-trial maneuvering proceeded, the Senate on May 29 declared by a vote of 37-29 that it had jurisdiction over Belknap regardless of his resignation. The trial, which ran from July 6 to Aug. 1, 1876, ended in acquittal, with 22 senators indicating that they had voted against conviction on the ground that the Senate lacked jurisdiction.

9. Name. Charles Swayne (1903-05). **Position.** Federal judge. **Charge.** Padding expense accounts; using railroad property in receivership for his personal benefit; misusing contempt power. **Decision.** Acquitted.

On Dec. 10, 1903, the House adopted a resolution for a Judiciary Committee investigation of Swayne, U.S. judge for the northern district of Florida. Months later, the committee recommended impeachment, and the House adopted the resolution by voice vote on Dec. 13, 1904. After the vote to impeach, 13 articles were drafted and approved by the House in 1905; however, only the first 12 articles were presented to the Senate. The Senate trial opened Feb. 10 and ended Feb. 27, when the Senate voted acquittal on all 12 articles.

10. Name. Robert W. Archbald (1912-1913). **Position.** Circuit judge, U.S. Commerce Court. **Charge.** Misconduct including personal profits, free trips to Europe, improper appointment of jury commissioner. **Decision.** Removed from office.

On May 4, 1912, the House adopted a Judiciary Committee resolution authorizing an investigation of Archbald, associate judge of the U.S. Commerce Court. A committee resolution impeaching Archbald and setting forth 13 articles of impeachment was adopted by the House July 11 by a 223-1 vote. The trial, which began Dec. 3, ended Jan. 13, 1913, with Archbald convicted on five of the 13 articles. The Senate on the same day removed him from office by voice vote and, by a 39-35 vote, disqualified him from further office.

11. Name. George W. English (1925-1926). **Position.** Federal judge. **Charge.** Partiality, tyranny and oppression. **Decision.** Senate dismissed charges at request of House managers following judge's resignation.

A resolution asking for an investigation of English, U.S. judge for the eastern district of Illinois, was introduced Jan. 13, 1925. The House on April 1, 1926, adopted by a 306-62 vote a Judiciary Committee resolution to impeach English. The resolution also set forth five articles of impeachment. The trial was set to begin Nov. 10, but on Nov. 4 English resigned, and, at the request of House managers the Senate dismissed the charges Dec. 13 by a vote of 70 to 9.

12. Name. Harold Louderback (1932-1933). **Position.** Federal judge. **Charge.** Appointing incompetent receivers and allowing them excessive fees. **Decision.** Acquitted.

On June 9, 1932, the House by voice vote adopted a resolution for an investigation of Louderback, U.S. judge for the northern district of California. The Judiciary Committee's study produced mixed results. The majority recommended censuring but not impeaching Louderback. However, the House on Feb. 24, 1933, by a 183-142 vote adopted a minority resolution impeaching the judge and specifying five articles. They accused Louderback of favoritism and conspiracy in the appointment of bankruptcy receivers. A trial that lasted from May 15 to May 24 ended in acquittal, with the "not guilty" votes outnumbering the "guilty" votes on all except one of the five articles.

13. Name. Halsted L. Ritter (1933-1936). **Position.** Federal judge. **Charge.** A variety of judicial improprieties, including receiving corrupt payments; practicing law while serving as a federal judge; preparing and filing false income tax returns. **Decision.** Removed from office.

On June 1, 1933, the House by voice vote adopted a resolution for an investigation of Ritter, U.S. judge for the southern district of Florida. A long delay followed. Then on March 2, 1936, the House by a 181-146 vote adopted a Judiciary Committee impeachment resolution, with four articles of impeachment (the four original articles were subsequently replaced with seven amended ones). The trial lasted from April 6 to April 17. Although there were more "guilty" than "not guilty" votes on all except one of the first six articles, the majorities fell short of the two-thirds required for conviction. However, on the seventh article, with 56 votes necessary for conviction, the vote was 56 guilty and 28 not guilty. Thus, Ritter was convicted. He was ordered removed from office without a vote. An order to disqualify him from further office was defeated, 0-76.

THE RULES OF IMPEACHMENT: A MATTER OF PRECEDENTS

What rules would guide House consideration of an impeachment resolution—and articles of impeachment? Under what rules would the Senate conduct the trial of a person impeached by the House?

The House has no standing rules dealing with its role in the impeachment process, a role which the Constitution describes in fewer than a dozen words: "The House of Representatives...shall have the sole power of impeachment." It is likely that when a specific recommendation of impeachment came to the House floor, the leadership might move to adopt ground rules to guide its consideration of the matter. If not, the standing rules of the House would apply, along with the precedents established by House action on other impeachments.

The Senate, on the other hand, adopted in 1868 for the impeachment trial of President Andrew Johnson, a set of 25 rules for such an event. One additional rule was adopted by the Senate in 1935. Many of the questions which might arise during a Senate trial can be answered by reference to this set of rules. *(Box p. 12)*

The Constitution too is more explicit about the Senate procedures for impeachment. It states that the Senate has "the sole power to try all impeachments," that when trying an impeachment, the senators should be under oath; that the Chief Justice should preside when the President is being tried; and that "no person shall be convicted without the concurrence of two-thirds of the members present."

Some of the questions about impeachment procedures can be answered, at least in part, by looking to precedent and the existing rules. Some of these follow:

On The House Side

Has the House always referred the matter of impeachment to a committee for an initial inquiry?

Yes. Before creation of the Judiciary Committee in 1813, the matter was referred to a special committee created for that purpose. This was the case in the first three impeachments, those of Sen. William Blount, Judge John Pickering and Justice Samuel Chase; the impeachment of Judge James H. Peck was the first referred to the Judiciary Committee.

The impeachment of President Andrew Johnson consisted of two attempts at impeachment: one in 1867 which went through the House Judiciary Committee, and a second one in 1868. In the second the evidence gathered by the Judiciary Committee was transmitted to the Committee on Reconstruction.

The impeachment of William W. Belknap, secretary of war, in 1876 arose from an investigation of his activities by the Committee on Expenditures in the War Department. The testimony taken by that committee was referred to the Judiciary Committee with instructions to prepare and report articles of impeachment without unnecessary delay.

Does the subject of an impeachment inquiry have the right to be present at the committee proceedings, to be represented by counsel to present witnesses and to question witnesses?

The answer to this question is up to the Judiciary Committee. It is "a matter of grace, not of right" for the person under investigation to be granted these privileges, House Judiciary Committee Chairman Peter W. Rodino Jr. (D N.J.) has said. The committee decides this matter in each case in which it arises.

During the first impeachment in which the Judiciary Committee recommended impeachment, Judge James H. Peck was allowed to be present in the committee room—a privilege of which he availed himself. He addressed the committee and cross-examined witnesses, although he was not permitted to introduce his own witnesses into the proceeding.

In the subsequent impeachment proceedings against Judge West H. Humphreys and President Andrew Johnson, the issue of their presence does not appear to have been raised. During the investigation by the Committee on Expenditures in the War Department which uncovered evidence against Secretary of War William W. Belknap, later impeached for those activities, Belknap was informed of the testimony against him by the chairman who read the adverse testimony to him. Upon Belknap's request, the committee granted him the privilege of employing counsel and cross-examining the witness against him. He was also granted permission to appear before the committee and deliver a sworn statement; he did not take advantage of this opportunity.

In subsequent impeachment inquiries, Judge Charles Swayne, Judge Robert W. Archbald, Judge Harold Louderback, and Judge Halsted Ritter were all allowed by the committee to be present at the public committee hearings. Swayne testified on his own behalf and was cross-examined. Archbald was allowed to be represented by counsel and to cross-examine witnesses. Louderback was also represented by counsel.

Is the committee's report on impeachment always accompanied by articles of impeachment?

No. In the impeachment of Sen. William Blount in 1797, the House impeached him, announced the impeachment to the Senate, and then appointed a select committee for the purpose of drawing up articles of impeachment. Congress recessed between impeachment and the presentation of the articles. The committee reported first the evidence against Blount and then, in early 1798, the articles, which the House approved.

This pattern—of impeachment and then the drawing up of the articles—was followed throughout the nineteenth century. In the impeachment of Judge John Pickering in 1803-1804, the House impeached Pickering, and Congress adjourned before the articles were drawn up. The new Congress convened and the House appointed a committee which drew up the articles.

Congressional Votes on Impeachment, 1797-1936

The following table shows the votes by which the 13 federal officials impeached prior to 1974 were impeached by the House, and the subsequent Senate votes on their case. The dates in parentheses are the dates on which the votes were taken.

The **series of votes** following some of the "guilty" or "not guilty" verdicts of the Senate are the **votes on each article of impeachment.** Although only a majority vote by the House is required to im-

peach, a two-thirds vote of guilty is required to convict on any article of impeachment. After a man was found guilty on any of the articles by a two-thirds vote, the Senate voted on whether to remove him from office—that vote carried by a majority. Sometimes the Senate has gone beyond that vote and voted on disqualifying the man from any future federal office; that vote too requires only majority approval.

	House	Senate		House	Senate
Blount	Voice (July 7, 1797)	**Dismissed,** 14-11 (Jan. 11, 1799)	Belknap	Voice (March 2, 1876)	**Not guilty,** 35-25, 36-25, 36-25, 36-25. 37-25. (Aug. 1, 1876)
Pickering	45-8 (March 2, 1803)	**Guilty,** 19-7, 19-7, 19-7, 19-7 **Removed** from office, 20-6 (March 12, 1804)	Swayne	Voice (Dec. 13, 1904)	**Not guilty,** 33-49, 32-50, 32-50, 13-69, 13-69, 31-51, 19-63, 31-51, 31-51, 31-51 31-51, 35-47. (Feb. 27, 1905)
Chase	73-32 (March 12, 1804)	**Not guilty,** 16-18, 10-24, 18-16, 18-16, 0-34 4-30, 10-24, 19-15 (March 1, 1805)			
Peck	123-49 (April 24, 1830)	**Not guilty,** 21-22 (Jan. 31, 1831)	Archbald	223-1 (July 11, 1912)	**Guilty,** 68-5, 46-25, 60-11, 52-20, 66-6, 24-45, 29-36, 22-42, 23-39, 1-65, 11-51, 19-46, 42-20. **Removed,** voice.
Humphreys	Voice (May 6, 1862)	**Guilty,** 39-0, 36-1, 33-4, 28-10, 39-0, 36-1 12-24, 35-1, 35-1 **Removed** from office, 38-0 **Disqualified** from future office, 36-0 (June 26, 1862)			**Disqualified,** 39-35 (Jan. 13, 1913)
			English	306-62 (April 1, 1926)	**Dismissed,** 70-9 (Dec. 13, 1926)
			Louderback	183-142 (Feb. 24, 1933)	**Not guilty,** 34-42, 23-47, 11-63, 30-47, 45-34 (May 24, 1933)
Johnson	57-108 against impeachment (Dec. 6, 1867)		Ritter	181-146 (March 2, 1936)	**Guilty,** 55-29, 52-32, 44-39, 36-48, 36-48 46-37, 56-28.
	126-47 for impeachment (Feb. 24, 1868)	**Not Guilty,** 35-19, 35-19, 35-19 (May 16, 26, 1868)			**Removed,** voice. **Not disqualified,** 0-76 against. (April 17, 1936)
Delahay	Voice (Feb. 28, 1873)	**None**			

Sources: *Impeachment: Selected Materials on Procedure*, House Committee on the Judiciary, January 1974; *Congressional Globe* 1868; Ritter data, *Congressional Record*. Vol. 80, April 17, 1936

Present practice, beginning with the impeachment of Judge Robert W. Archbald in 1912, has been that the committee simultaneously reports out both a resolution of impeachment and articles of impeachment.

Can the House vote to impeach someone if the committee recommends against impeachment?

Yes. The House is no more bound by a committee's recommendation on impeachment than it is by a committee recommendation and action on any legislative matter.

After investigating the evidence against Judge Harold Louderback in 1932-33, the committee found circumstances and evidence insufficient to warrant impeachment—and recommended adoption of a resolution to that effect. A minority of the committee dissented and proposed articles of impeachment. When the matter

came to the House floor, the House approved a substitute amendment which included the articles of impeachment—and impeached the judge. He was later found not guilty by the Senate.

Can the House make changes in the articles of impeachment as reported from the committee?

Yes. During the impeachment of Justice Samuel Chase in 1804, the House in the Committee of the Whole considered and adopted amendments to the articles of impeachment. The House later disapproved all the amendments added in the Committee of the Whole and approved the articles as reported from the select committee.

When the articles of impeachment against President Johnson were considered in 1868 by the full House, two additional articles were suggested by the persons chosen

(Continued on p. 14)

Senate Rules of Procedure and Practice...

Following are the major provisions of rules used by the Senate during impeachment trials. With the exception of Rule XI, which was adopted May 28, 1935, the rules have remained unchanged since their adoption March 2, 1868, for the trial of President Johnson.

I. Whensoever the Senate shall receive notice from the House of Representatives that managers are appointed on their part to conduct an impeachment against any person and are directed to carry articles of impeachment to the Senate, the Secretary of the Senate shall immediately inform the House of Representatives that the Senate is ready to receive the managers for the purpose of exhibiting such articles of impeachment, agreeably to such notice.

II. When the managers of an impeachment shall be introduced at the bar of the Senate and shall signify that they are ready to exhibit articles of impeachment against any person, the Presiding Officer of the Senate shall direct the Sergeant at Arms to make proclamation...after which the articles shall be exhibited, and then the Presiding Officer of the Senate shall inform the managers that the Senate will take proper order on the subject of the impeachment, of which due notice shall be given to the House of Representatives.

III. Upon such articles being presented to the Senate, the Senate shall, at 1 o'clock afternoon of the day (Sunday excepted) following such presentation, or sooner if ordered by the Senate, proceed to the consideration of such articles and shall continue in session from day to day (Sundays excepted) after the trial shall commence (unless otherwise ordered by the Senate) until final judgment shall be rendered, and so much longer as may, in its judgment, be needful. Before proceeding to the consideration of the articles of impeachment, the Presiding Officer shall administer the oath hereinafter provided to the members of the Senate then present and to the other members of the Senate as they shall appear, whose duty it shall be to take the same.

IV. When the President of the United States or the Vice President of the United States, upon whom the powers and duties of the office of President shall have devolved, shall be impeached, the Chief Justice of the Supreme Court of the United States shall preside; and in a case requiring the said Chief Justice to preside notice shall be given to him by the Presiding Officer of the Senate of the time and place fixed for the consideration of the articles of impeachment, as aforesaid, with a request to attend; and the said Chief Justice shall preside over the Senate during the consideration of said articles and upon the trial of the person impeached therein.

V. The Presiding Officer shall have power to make and issue, by himself or by the Secretary of the Senate, all orders, mandates, writs, and precepts authorized by these rules or by the Senate, and to make and enforce such other regulations and orders in the premises as the Senate may authorize or provide.

VI. The Senate shall have power to compel the attendance of witnesses, to enforce obedience to its orders, mandates, writs, precepts, and judgments, to preserve order, and to punish in a summary way contempts of, and disobedience to, its authority, orders, mandates, writs, precepts, or judgments, and to make all lawful orders, rules, and regulations which it may deem essential or conducive to the ends of justice And the Sergeant at Arms, under the direction of the Senate, may employ such aid and assistance as may be necessary to enforce, execute and carry into effect the lawful orders, mandates, writs, and precepts of the Senate.

VII. The Presiding Officer of the Senate shall direct necessary preparations in the Senate Chamber, and the Presiding Officer on the trial shall direct all the forms of proceedings while the Senate is sitting for the purpose of trying an impeachment, and all forms during the trial not otherwise specially provided for. And the Presiding Officer on the trial may rule all questions of evidence and incidental questions, which ruling shall stand as the judgment of the Senate, unless some member of the Senate shall ask that a formal vote be taken thereon, in which case it shall be submitted to the Senate for decision; or he may at his option, in the first instance, submit any such question to a vote of the members of the Senate. Upon all such questions the vote shall be without a division, unless the yeas and nays be demanded by one-fifth of the members present, when the same shall be taken.

VII. Upon the presentation of articles of impeachment and the organization of the Senate as herein before provided, a writ of summons shall issue to the accused, reciting said articles, and notifying him to appear before the Senate upon a day and at a place to be fixed by the Senate and named in such writ, and file his answer to said articles of impeachment, and to stand to and abide the orders and judgments of the Senate thereon; which writ shall be served by such officer or person as shall be named in the precept thereof, such number of days prior to the day fixed for such appearance as shall be named in such precept, either by the delivery of an attested copy thereof to the person accused, or if that can not conveniently be done, by leaving such copy at the last known place of abode of such person, or at his usual place of business in some conspicuous place therein; or if such service shall be, in the judgment of the Senate, impracticable, notice to the accused to appear shall be given in such other manner, by publication or otherwise, as shall be deemed just; and if the writ aforesaid shall fail of service in the manner aforesaid, the proceedings shall not thereby abate, but further service may be made in such manner as the Senate shall direct. If the accused, after service, shall fail to appear, either in person or by attorney, on the day so fixed therefor as aforesaid, or, appearing, shall fail to file his answer to such articles of impeachment, the trial shall proceed, nevertheless, as upon a plea of not guilty. If a plea of guilty shall be entered, judgment may be entered thereon without further proceedings.

IX. At 12:30 o'clock afternoon of the day appointed for the return of the summons against the person impeached, the legislative and executive business of the Senate shall be suspended, and the Secretary of the Senate shall administer an oath to the returning officer.... Which oath shall be entered at large on the records.

X. The person impeached shall then be called to appear and answer the articles of impeachment against him. If he appear, or any person for him, the appearance shall be recorded, stating particularly if by himself, or by agent or

...When Sitting for Impeachment Trials

attorney, naming the person appearing and the capacity in which he appears. If he does not appear, either personally or by agent or attorney, the same shall be recorded.

XI. That in the trial of any impeachment the Presiding Officer of the Senate, upon the order of the Senate, shall appoint a committee of twelve Senators to receive evidence and take testimony at such times and places as the committee may determine, and for such purpose the committee so appointed and the chairman thereof, to be elected by the committee, shall (unless otherwise ordered by the Senate) exercise all the powers and functions conferred upon the Senate and the Presiding Officer of the Senate, respectively, under the rules of procedure and practice in the Senate when sitting on impeachment trials.

Unless otherwise ordered by the Senate, the rules of procedure and practice in the Senate when sitting on impeachment trials shall govern the procedure and practice of the committee so appointed. The committee so appointed shall report to the Senate in writing a certified copy of the transcript of the proceedings and testimony had and given before such committee, and such report shall be received by the Senate and the evidence so received and the testimony so taken shall be considered to all intents and purposes, subject to the right of the Senate to determine competency, relevancy, and materiality, as having been received and taken before the Senate, but nothing herein shall prevent the Senate from sending for any witness and hearing his testimony in open Senate, or by order of the Senate having the entire trial in open Senate.

XII. At 12:30 o'clock afternoon of the day appointed for the trial of an impeachment, the legislative and executive business of the Senate shall be suspended, and the Secretary shall give notice to the House of Representatives that the Senate is ready to proceed upon the impeachment of— in the Senate Chamber, which chamber is prepared with accommodations for the reception of the House of Representatives.

XIII. The hour of the day at which the Senate shall sit upon the trial of an impeachment shall be (unless otherwise ordered) 12 o'clock p.m.; and when the hour for such thing shall arrive, the Presiding Officer of the Senate shall so announce; and thereupon the Presiding Officer upon such trial shall cause proclamation to be made, and the business of the trial shall proceed. The adjournment of the Senate sitting in said trial shall not operate as an adjournment of the Senate; but on such adjournment the Senate shall resume the consideration of its legislative and executive business.

XIV. The Secretary of the Senate shall record the proceedings in cases of impeachment as in the case of legislative proceedings, and the same shall be reported in the same manner as the legislative proceedings of the Senate.

XV. Counsel for the parties shall be admitted to appear and be heard upon an impeachment.

XVI. All motions made by the parties or their counsel shall be addressed to the Presiding Officer, and if he, or any Senator, shall require it, they shall be committed to writing, and read at the Secretary's table.

XVII. Witnesses shall be examined by one person on behalf of the party producing them, and then cross-examined by one person on the other side.

XVIII. If a Senator is called as a witness, he shall be sworn, and give his testimony standing in his place.

XIX. If a Senator wishes a question to be put to a witness, or to offer a motion or order (except a motion to adjourn), it shall be reduced to writing, and put by the Presiding Officer.

XX. At all times while the Senate is sitting upon the trial of an impeachment the doors of the Senate shall be kept open, unless the Senate shall direct the doors to be closed while deliberating upon its decisions.

XXI. All preliminary or interlocutory questions, and all motions, shall be argued for not exceeding one hour on each side, unless the Senate shall, by order, extend the time.

XXII. The case, on each side, shall be opened by one person. The final argument on the merits may be made by two persons on each side (unless otherwise ordered by the Senate upon application for that purpose), and the argument shall be opened and closed on the part of the House of Representatives.

XXIII. On the final question whether the impeachment is sustained, the yeas and nays shall be taken on each article of impeachment separately; and if the impeachment shall not, upon any of the articles presented, be sustained by the votes of two-thirds of the members present, a judgment of acquittal shall be entered; but if the person accused in such articles of impeachment shall be convicted upon any of said articles by the votes of two-thirds of the members present, the Senate shall proceed to pronounce judgment, and a certified copy of such judgment shall be deposited in the office of the Secretary of State.

XXIV. All the orders and decisions shall be made and had by yeas and nays, which shall be entered on the record, and without debate, subject, however, to the operation of Rule VII, except when the doors shall be closed for deliberation, and in that case no member shall speak more than once on one question, and for not more than ten minutes on an interlocutory question, and for not more than fifteen minutes on the final question, unless by consent of the Senate, to be had without debate; but a motion to adjourn may be decided without the yeas and nays, unless they be demanded by one-fifth of the members present. The fifteen minutes herein allowed shall be for the whole deliberation on the final question, and not on the final question on each article of impeachment.

XXV. Witnesses shall be sworn.... Which oath shall be administered by the Secretary, or any other duly authorized person.

All process shall be served by the Sergeant at Arms of the Senate, unless otherwise ordered by the court.

XXVI. If the Senate shall at any time fail to sit for the consideration of articles of impeachment on the day or hour fixed therefor, the Senate may, by an order to be adopted without debate, fix a day and hour for resuming such consideration.

(Continued from p. 11)

as managers of the impeachment trial, and the House adopted them.

Does the House vote separately on the matter of impeachment and on the articles of impeachment?

Yes. Usually the House resolves itself into the Committee of the Whole to consider the report of the committee. After debating it there and discussing amendments, the committee rises and asks the House to concur in adoption of the resolution of impeachment. There is a vote, usually a roll-call vote, on the resolution, and then a vote on the articles of impeachment, individually or as a unit. Only a majority is required to approve a resolution of impeachment and to approve articles of impeachment. *(Votes, box p. 11)*

The House may vote to table the report on impeachment but that vote does not preclude reconsideration of the impeachment of the individual concerned in the report. It does preclude reconsideration of that particular report.

How does the House officially notify the Senate that it has impeached someone?

After voting to impeach, the House appoints a small committee—usually composed of two of the leaders of the committee recommending impeachment—to inform the Senate of the House action. They walk over and announce the matter to the Senate.

In 1868, after the House voted to impeach President Johnson, Reps. Thaddeus Stevens (R Pa.) and John A. Bingham (R Ohio) appeared before the Senate and proclaimed: "We appear before you and in the name of the House of Representatives and of all the people of the United States we do impeach Andrew Johnson, president of the United States, of high crimes and misdemeanors in office!"

More recently, the House has simply sent a message to the Senate to notify it of its action—and then the chairman of the House managers, appearing later before the Senate, has announced the impeachment aloud.

On the Senate Side

Who presents the case for impeachment to the Senate?

The managers for the House, men selected by the House after the impeachment vote, to serve as the prosecutors of the case in the Senate. An odd number—from five to 11—has traditionally been selected, including members of both parties, all of whom supported impeachment. They have been selected in various ways—by ballot, with a majority vote necessary for election; by resolution naming the slate; or by the Speaker when he is so authorized by the House.

The managers select their own chairman. There is no mention of the managers in the Constitution, and no requirement that they be members of the House. It is therefore possible that members of the committee staff conducting the impeachment inquiry could be named as managers along with some members of the House.

What sort of proceedings can intervene in an impeachment between the House vote to impeach and the beginning of the Senate trial?

Before the trial formally begins the person impeached may demur to the charges—claiming either that he is not one of the persons subject to impeachment or that the charges against him are not the constitutional

grounds for impeachment—"treason, bribery, or other high crimes and misdemeanors."

After he or his counsel presents this claim, the managers on the part of the House may prepare a response, which must be submitted to the House for its approval. If approved, it is submitted to the Senate. This process may continue at length—with the impeached person responding again, the House managers again, etc. The Senate decides the matter after all the arguments are filed.

What are the powers of the presiding officer in a Senate impeachment trial?

The presiding officer—the Chief Justice in the case of the impeachment of the President or Vice President—can issue all orders needed to compel witnesses to appear or to enforce obedience to Senate orders. The presiding officer administers the oath to all the senators before they take part in the trial.

The presiding officer rules on all questions of evidence and his ruling stands unless he decides to submit the question to a vote of the Senate, or unless a senator requests such a vote. Custom dictates that most questions concerning the admissibility of evidence are submitted to the Senate for decision.

The presiding officer questions witnesses, often asking questions submitted to him in writing by various senators, who do not directly question witnesses themselves. All questions which senators ask—of managers, counsel, or witnesses—must be in writing.

Can both sides call witnesses in an impeachment trial?

Yes. Both sides can call witnesses, examine them, and cross-examine witnesses for the other side. The impeached person may also testify in his own behalf.

What votes does the Senate take in an impeachment trial?

All orders and decisions made by the Senate in an impeachment trial are by roll-call vote, and without debate—unless in secret session. On the final question in impeachment—guilt or innocence—each senator is limited to 15 minutes of debate in secret session.

The Senate casts roll-call votes on each article of impeachment; a two-thirds vote is needed for conviction. If no article receives the approval of two-thirds of the members present, the impeached official is found not guilty. If any article receives two-thirds approval, he is found guilty. The Senate then votes to remove him from office—and, if desired, votes on whether to disqualify him from holding future offices.

How long does the process of impeachment take—from the House vote to impeach to the Senate vote to convict or acquit?

The shortest time from House impeachment to Senate verdict was one month—in the last impeachment—that of Federal Judge Halsted Ritter in 1936. The longest time was one year—in the early impeachments of Pickering and Chase. The impeachment of Andrew Johnson took three months from House action to Senate judgment. *(Box, p. 4)*

The shortest Senate trial on record is that of Judge West H. Humphreys—which took only one day; the longest was the two months consumed in the Senate trial of President Johnson.

(Continued on p. 30)

ANATOMY OF A COMMITTEE: IMPEACHMENT INQUIRY BEGINS

"A well-constituted court for the trial of impeachments is an object not more to be desired than difficult to be obtained in a government wholly elective. The subjects of its jurisdiction are those offenses which proceed from the misconduct of public men...from the abuse or violation of some public trust...which may with peculiar propriety be denominated POLITICAL.... The prosecution of them...will seldom fail to agitate the passions of the whole community, and to divide it into parties more or less friendly or inimical to the accused. In many cases it will connect itself with the pre-existing factions, and will enlist all their animosities, partialities, influence and interest on one side or the other; and in such cases there will always be the greatest danger that the decision will be regulated more by the comparative strength of the parties than by the real demonstrations of innocence or guilt."

—Alexander Hamilton in *The Federalist Papers,*
No. 65

Peter Rodino, New Jersey Democrat, hoped to prove Alexander Hamilton, founding father, wrong in 1974.

In 1787, 56 years before the first presidential impeachment attempt, Hamilton warned that an impeachment would invariably erupt in partisan dispute. Rodino, on the other hand, repeatedly warned that it would be a national disaster if the impeachment inquiry currently underway in the House Judiciary Committee, which he heads, becomes a partisan matter. *(Box p. 18)*

But since Oct. 23, 1973, when the committee was formally granted jurisdiction over the inquiry into charges against President Nixon, the grim prospect of impeachment threatened the committee's traditional nonpartisan comity. As 1974 began, few persons were more aware of the dangers which Alexander Hamilton had predicted than the 38 lawyers who compose the committee.

'The Judicious Committee'

"The Judiciary Committee likes to think of itself as the judicious committee," said Edward Hutchinson (R Mich.), the committee's ranking Republican. But that judiciousness has been jeopardized already by the actions which led committee member David W. Dennis (R Ind.) to note that "the chairman has been running this inquiry pretty much out of his hat."

"We in the minority have been given no real opportunity to participate or be informed," protested Wiley Mayne (R Ind.) in November, as he and other Republicans moved to postpone House approval of $1-million to fund the committee inquiry.

Acutely sensitized to the effect their part in presidential impeachment might have on their own political fortunes, Republican committee members were anxious to be kept informed about what was going on—and to have some role in deciding what should be done. "What is at issue," said freshman Republican Harold V. Froehlich (R Wis.), "is letting the minority participate.... Let us know what is what, and let us know what is going on."

"All we can do is complain," conceded Robert McClory (R Ill.), second-ranking Republican on the committee. "We don't have the votes to override whatever the majority decides to do."

And complain was what McClory did, leading 10 of the other Republican committee members for an hour Dec. 18, 1973, from the floor of the House.

An Impeachable Offense Is....

✓ ..."treason, bribery, or other high crimes and misdemeanors."—*The Constitution*

✓ ..."one in its nature or consequences subversive of some fundamental or essential principle of government, or highly prejudicial to the public interest...a violation of the Constitution, of law, of an official oath, or of duty, by an act committed or omitted, or, without violating a positive law, by the abuse of discretionary powers from improper motives, or for any improper motives, or for any improper purpose."—*Benjamin F. Butler* (R Mass.), one of the House managers of the impeachment case against Andrew Johnson, March 30, 1868

✓ ..."of such a character to commend itself at once to the minds of all right thinking men, as beyond all question, an adequate cause (for impeachment). It should...leave no reasonable ground of suspicion upon the motives of those who inflict the penalty...."—*William Pitt Fessenden* (Whig Maine), one of the seven "Republicans" in the Senate who voted against the conviction of Andrew Johnson

✓ ...actions "as an individual and such judge.... (which brought) his court into scandal and disrepute, to the prejudice of said court and public confidence in the administration of justice therein, and to the prejudice of public respect and confidence in the federal judiciary and to render him unfit to serve as such judge."—*Articles of Impeachment against Federal District Judge Halsted Ritter,* 1936

✓ ..."whatever a majority of the House of Representatives considers it to be at a given moment in history; conviction results from whatever offenses two-thirds of the other body considers to be sufficiently serious to require removal of the accused from office.... There are few fixed principles among the handful of precedents."—*Rep. Gerald R. Ford,* speech on the House floor, April 15, 1970

" 'Consultation' according to the chairman," lamented McClory, "seems to mean reporting to the committee members decisions which the chairman has already made. That really is not consultation."

The following day, Dec. 19, Rodino assembled the seven senior members of both parties on the committee and informed them that they were an advisory group for the inquiry. Alluding vaguely to their 'supervisory' role, Rodino left their responsibilities undefined.

Doar Appointment. Creation of—and their inclusion in—the advisory group encouraged the committee Republicans, but their feelings were still somewhat ruffled as the session ended just before Christmas. Rodino had singlehandedly selected John M. Doar, a former assistant attorney general for civil rights under the Kennedy and Johnson administrations, as the committee's special impeachment counsel. No other committee members were informed of Rodino's choice before the public announcement, except for Hutchinson, to whom Rodino introduced Doar the previous afternoon.

"There are some Democrats on the committee who would vote to impeach Nixon today. And there are a few Republicans who wouldn't vote to impeach Nixon if he were caught in a bank vault at midnight."

—William L. Hungate (D Mo.)

Despite Doar's background as a Republican, Hutchinson and McClory made it clear that his ties to the Kennedy family were of concern to them. At the Dec. 20 press conference announcing Doar's appointment, Hutchinson, at the request of one of Rodino's aides, sat at the small table with Rodino and Doar. But he moved his chair down to one end, out of camera range, and turned to the side, making clear that he was an onlooker, not a participant in the announcement.

Equal Footing. But a two-hour meeting early in January of the advisory group with Doar, who presented his first progress report, and the naming of Albert E. Jenner, a distinguished trial attorney, as minority counsel for the inquiry, bolstered the confidence of Republican members.

Now, they indicated, they felt themselves on a more equal footing with their Democratic colleagues on the slippery subject of impeaching the President. *(Doar, Jenner staff, p. 31)*

And yet committee comity faced severe strains in the early months of 1974. A number of questions demanding committee attention were certain to arouse partisan suspicions and tensions anew. These included: the committee's relationship to the special prosecutor, the proper manner of exercising subpoena power in the inquiry, the limitations of the areas of the inquiry, the timetable for the inquiry, and the definition of an impeachable offense.

A Reputation to Preserve

The committee's reputation as one of the least partisan in the House was a matter of quiet pride for most of its members, virtually all of whom indicated a desire to preserve that reputation through the impeachment inquiry, and beyond. When questioned concerning the committee and the inquiry, most members chose their words carefully to avoid any aggravation of the already building tension.

"We're all lawyers," Dennis and several other members pointed out, noting one major factor which has worked to create this reputation for nonpartisanship. The shared professional background, members noted, would hopefully encourage a "lawyer-like" approach to the inquiry.

"There are some Democrats on the committee who would vote to impeach Nixon today," admitted William L. Hungate (D Mo.). "And there are a few Republicans who wouldn't vote to impeach Nixon if he were caught in a bank vault at midnight. But the majority (of the members) will, I hope, decide the matter on the basis of the evidence presented."

Past Leadership. Another element in the committee's reputation was the legacy of a unique leadership team—Emanuel Celler (D N.Y. 1923-1973) and William M. McCulloch (R Ohio 1947-1973), who served as chairman and ranking minority member together from 1959 until both left the House at the end of 1972. They saw eye-to-eye on many of the issues which came before the committee during those years, a coincidence of views which contributed to bipartisan support of most measures emerging from the committee, and one which left dissenting Republicans on the committee out in the cold, and leaderless.

Legal Matters. Still a third influence was the subject matter which generally fell within the committee's jurisdiction. As Charles E. Wiggins (R Calif.) reflected: "The jurisdiction of the committee has tended to shield it from partisan controversy." If disagreement arises over bankruptcy, civil liberties, constitutional amendments, federal courts and judges, immigration, prisons or patents, it is more likely to reflect philosophical rather than party differences.

Hutchinson agreed: "In the ordinary course of committee work, the great bulk of the matters coming before the committee are more legal than political.... There have been extremely few issues that end up being partisanly political."

Philosophical Gap. The philosophical cleavage in the committee appeared to be widening, however. As Walter Flowers (D Ala.), one of the more conservative Democrats on the committee, described it: "The committee make-up doesn't really reflect the make-up of the House: the Democrats are more liberal than the Democrats in the House as a whole, the (committee) leadership in particular, and the Republicans are more conservative than the Republicans in the House as a whole."

Voting studies by Congressional Quarterly supported his observation: in 1973 the average House Democrat supported President Nixon on 35 per cent of the votes—while the average Democrat on the committee supported him less frequently, on only 31 per cent of the votes. The same year, the average Republican on the committee supported the President on 64 per cent of the votes, more often than the average Republican in the House, whose record was 62 per cent. *(Voting study p. 42)*

Democrats held 21 of the 38 seats on the committee. As the 1974 session began, there was a vacancy in one of the 17 Republican seats, left by the resignation of William J. Keating (R Ohio 1971-1974) in January. The Republican Committee on Committees selected Delbert L. Latta (Ohio) as his replacement on the committee on Feb. 13.

The 38 members represented districts in 21 states, from Maine to California. Three were black; two were women. Six were in their thirties; half were younger than 50, and five were older than 60.

A Year of Changes

The 1972 election returns contained drastic changes for the House Judiciary Committee. The departure of the Celler-McCulloch team moved into leadership posts two men little known outside the House and untried as leaders. As power, released from Celler's tight grasp, was diffused, some of the more junior committee members began to emerge as influential figures.

Also, 11 freshmen were added to the committee in 1973. Including the six members who first had been elected in 1970, the committee wound up with almost half its members elected for the first time within the last four years.

The Leaders. Caution marked Rodino's move to the chair occupied for decades by one of the House's strongest committee leaders, caution which drew criticism. Late in 1973 a freshman Republican complained of the committee's lack of direction; another member remarked, with a resigned air, of Rodino's ability to be "firmly indecisive." Others attributed this characteristic to Rodino's effort to accommodate a range of individual views on the Democratic side—from conservative members like Flowers and James R. Mann (D S.C.) to vociferous liberals like John Conyers Jr. (D Mich.) and Robert Drinan (D Mass.). "I don't think that he can control his troops as well as he might," one Republican remarked.

"Pete is trying very hard to conduct this (impeachment inquiry) right," another one said later, "but he is riding a real bucking horse on his side, and the Republicans are not making things any easier, I guess."

"Peter is not an institution; Celler was," noted a Democrat, adding that he and others had been pleasantly surprised by the leadership ability Rodino had shown in his first year as chairman.

Most members felt that they had more input into committee decisions under Rodino's more democratic rule, although one senior Democrat warned that the change might be more of style than of substance: "Rodino gives the appearance of softer leadership, but in fact he exercises a strong hand," he said, noting that Rodino had acted alone in the selection of special counsel Doar.

Hutchinson, a quiet man with a ponderous manner, also was criticized by some of his more activist colleagues who saw his low profile as evidence of distaste for his leadership post. Advising against any underestimation of the man, a committee Democrat recalled that, when Hutchinson served in the Michigan legislature before coming to the House, "he practically ran the state.... He knows what he is doing." And McClory praised Hutchin-

---

Potential Prosecutors

One little-known fact was likely to make even the most vigorous supporter of impeachment on the House Judiciary Committee carefully examine the evidence assembled to support impeachment charges against President Nixon: any member could end up prosecuting that case for impeachment before the Senate, and the nation. And—as ranking committee Republican Edward Hutchinson (R Mich.) told Congressional Quarterly— "if the first phase (the staff investigation) is not done well, the managers of impeachment in the Senate will find themselves left up the creek without a paddle."

After the impeachment is announced to the Senate, the case against the president traditionally has been presented and 'prosecuted' by House members. After the House votes to impeach, these "managers of impeachment" are selected—by ballot, by resolution, or by the speaker. In the past, the number selected has varied from five to 11—members from both parties who voted for impeachment. Once selected, they choose their own chairman.

The managers present the Senate the articles of impeachment. The chairman then impeaches the person to be tried, by accusing him orally before the Senate of the charges. Then the trial begins, and the House managers act as prosecutors of the impeachment case, examining witnesses and presenting evidence.

---

son for his leadership of the committee's Republicans: under him the Republicans on the committee were more cohesive than they had been in a decade, he said.

Hutchinson viewed his role as a coordinator of equals, not a director of strategy. He attempted "to work with the minority to formulate or ascertain what the minority views are on major legislation. And in that role, my policy has been to meet with Republican members very frequently, sometimes as often as once a week—not as a caucus so much as a forum for finding out what each other is thinking."

Next in Line. The House Judiciary Committee in 1973 was no longer under the close control of the finely honed working relationship between Celler and McCulloch. As Rodino and Hutchinson, vastly different men with dissimilar styles, began learning to work together in their new roles, power spread beyond them into the ranks of the committee.

During the year several of the other committee members in both parties gained stature as significant figures, whose contributions were influential in committee deliberations. Among those on the Democratic side were Jack Brooks of Texas, Robert W. Kastenmeier of Wisconsin and Hungate; on the Republican side—McClory, Tom Railsback of Illinois, Wiggins and Dennis. All were included as members of the impeachment advisory group. *(Profiles of all members, p. 21)*

Brooks, 51, a blunt and outspoken liberal with 22 years of service in the House, was considered talented and forceful by his colleagues. He played a lesser role than he might in Judiciary Committee deliberations as a whole, devoting more time to the Government Operations

Subcommittee which he chairs and which in 1973 investigated federal spending on Nixon's homes at San Clemente and Key Biscayne.

Kastenmeier, at 49, a veteran of 15 years' service in the House, was a liberal who headed the Judiciary Subcommittee on Courts, Civil Liberties, and the Administration of Justice. Hungate, 51, a moderate midwesterner, won his colleagues' praise in 1973 for the hard work his subcommittee put in on the complex federal rules of evidence, and on the special prosecutor measures.

On the Republican side, McClory, of equal seniority with Hutchinson and, except for the luck of the draw, ranking minority member himself, spoke out more and more often for the minority. Railsback, a moderate young member also from Illinois and fifth ranking on the committee, also was heard and seen more frequently voicing Republican members' concerns. Reports of friction between the two, and of McClory's resentment of Railback's assertiveness, were said by other committee members to be exaggerated.

Less outspoken but highly respected was Wiggins of California, considered by many the best legal mind on the committee. And Dennis of Indiana was praised by members on both sides for his "feisty" independence.

The Freshmen. Frustration about his role as a freshman member of the committee was voiced by Trent Lott (R Miss.), but most of the new members agreed with Elizabeth Holtzman's (D N.Y.) description of the committee leadership as "very open, receptive and fair" in dealing with the freshmen. Acknowledged stand-outs in their first year on the committee were Holtzman and Barbara Jordan (Texas) on the Democratic side and William S. Cohen of Maine among the Republicans.

A Time of Tension

Events conspired late in 1973 to place two historic tasks before this unpracticed committee.

In early October Vice President Spiro T. Agnew resigned; two days later, his successor—Rep. Gerald R. Ford (R Mich.)—was nominated. The House Judiciary Committee was designated to investigate the nomination, the first made under the Twenty-Fifth Amendment.

But before the hearings could begin, the Watergate tapes crisis had culminated in the firing of special prosecutor Archibald Cox and the introduction of more than 20 measures calling for an impeachment investigation. On Oct. 23, House Speaker Carl Albert (D Okla.) said he would refer all impeachment bills to the House Judiciary Committee. Referral to that committee was not automatic; impeachment is not listed in the House Rules as falling within the jurisdiction of that or any other committee.

"This cannot be a partisan effort," said Rodino Oct. 29, referring to the impeachment inquiry. But the following day, when the committee first met to discuss procedures for the inquiry regarding the Ford nomination and impeachment, partisan sensitivities flared.

One-Man Subpoena Power. The first skirmish came on Rodino's request that the committee delegate to him alone the power to subpoena witnesses and documents for these two inquiries. This would prevent delay, he said, by precluding the necessity of his calling the full committee together to approve each subpoena.

Tyler Impeachment Attempt

John Tyler, one of the most unpopular presidents in history, was the target of the first attempt to impeach a president. Ostracized by both major parties after moving up to the presidency on the death of William Henry Harrison, Tyler was saved from impeachment when the House Jan. 10, 1843, rejected a resolution proposing an investigation into his possible impeachment.

Wary of the potential of "one-man subpoena power," the Republicans countered with a suggestion that this power be exercised jointly by Rodino and Hutchinson. Cohen urged adoption of this alternative: compared to questions down the road this was an easy matter, and if the subpoenas were issued jointly, they would be less vulnerable to partisan attack, he contended. Approval of the alternative, he later said, would have been basically symbolic. Hutchinson's objection to a subpoena always could have been overridden by the full committee.

But Rodino opposed the suggestion, apparently viewing it as a challenge to his leadership. The Republican move was rejected on a straight party-line vote, 17-21; Rodino's request then was granted by another party vote, 21-17. Rodino said he would consult fully with Hutchinson on each subpoena, a promise which satisfied Cohen and some of the other Republicans. But the partisan animus aroused by the matter remained alive.

As Wiggins later commented: "The chairman states unequivocally that he wants to be fair. But as soon as the minority tries to require fair treatment in terms of the staff or subpoena power, the majority rises up, and by a staright party-line vote, rebuffs that effort."

Ford and the Prosecutor. That concern was not allayed by the partisan divisions which surfaced on the Ford confirmation vote in the House, and on the matter of authorizing a court-appointed special prosecutor.

Although there were Republican complaints of footdragging before the House hearings on the Ford nomination began, Rodino's conduct of the hearings once they were underway won high praise for their fairness. But when the House confirmed Ford Dec. 6, nine of the 35 negative votes were cast by Democrats on the Judiciary Committee.

Most surprising of these votes was Rodino's, which he explained on the floor as a response to the needs of his district. Republicans criticized the vote as partisan and strictly political, dictated by the political insecurity of a white man who represented a predominantly black constituency.

On the matter of a special prosecutor, the full committee rejected a Republican measure which would have left the prosecutor within the executive branch by a vote of 17-21—down party lines except that one Democrat (Flowers) and one Republican (Froehlich) switched sides.

One Million Dollars. 1973, as the committee began the Ford hearings Nov. 15, a resolution was introduced on the House floor granting the committee an additional $1-million to finance the impeachment inquiry. Anxious for answers to some preliminary questions about the inquiry, Republican members sought a delay of House action on the matter.

"Do the members realize," asked Wiggins, "that the committee...has not had its first meeting on the subject of impeachment? We have not yet decided what we are going to do, what is impeachable, what is not, and what instructions are to be given this staff?....Would it not be more fair and judicious and prudent for the committee to decide itself what we are going to do before we run to the House administration for money?"

McClory urged that the resolution be postponed until the Judiciary Committee could be called together to discuss plans for the inquiry.

Rodino protested that the Republicans were creating partisan feeling by their complaints. "Only yesterday, in addressing myself to a query...as to what might happen if this were not a bipartisan effort," Rodino noted, "I said it would be disastrous for the country."

A motion to kill the resolution by recommitting it failed by only 37 votes; the only Republicans on the committee who opposed recommittal were Cohen and Railsback. The House then approved the $1-million.

Problems of Procedure

Aware that the rules governing and limiting the impeachment inquiry would have substantial impact on its outcome, Republican members began pressing in December, 1973, for decisions on a variety of procedural matters. After one informal committee meeting and an hour of voicing their concerns from the House floor, they had, by Dec. 22, won establishment of the advisory group and a general target date of April for the end of the committee's work.

But a variety of unresolved procedural matters were certain to provoke intense discussion when the committee resumed its work after Jan. 21.

Even the procedural matters divided the committee along party lines. As Wiggins reflected: "It is the desire and the political interest of the majority to not have rules, so that there can be the broadest possible range for the investigation. But the interest of the law and the minority are served by deciding the rules first."

The Timetable. The need for some time limit was one of the first matters broached by the Republicans. Ralph Nader, not known to be a Republican ally in this matter, already had criticized the committee for dilly-dallying. Rodino was "suffering a crisis of a lack of self-confidence," he said, warning that "if the House does not vote impeachment by March, there will be none."

Nevertheless, Rodino Dec. 11 rebuffed Republican suggestions that the committee continue work in January during the recess in order to expedite its decision.

But Republicans persisted, interpreting Democratic resistance as calculated to delay a final decision on impeachment until election season. If there was no vote by April, Vice President Ford said Dec. 13, "then you can say it's partisan." And committee member Hamilton Fish Jr. (R N.Y.) warned a few days later: "The closer we get to the 1974 elections, and the further...from the events which generated this in-

quiry, the more likely whatever we do will be described as partisan."

Although a number of committee Democrats found March a reasonable target date, Rodino just before adjournment in December agreed that the committee should be finished by April. He made it clear that this was a hope more than a promise, and by Jan. 7, the target date had become "the latter part of April."

A Select Group. Concerned also about supervision of the staff working on the inquiry, Republicans pressed Rodino to appoint a select subcommittee to conduct certain phases of the investigation. Such a body had been created in 1970 to investigate impeachment charges against Supreme Court Justice William O. Douglas.

"All we can do is complain. We don't have the votes to override whatever the majority decides to do."

—Robert McClory (R Ill.)

"The full committee is too large a body to direct any project," said Hutchinson, who advocated that the Nixon impeachment charges also be handled by a small subcommittee. On Dec. 11, committee members apparently agreed on the need for a subcommittee, but failed to reach consensus on what precisely the subcommittee should do.

Railsback, one of the subcommittee proposal's chief proponents, would have the subcommittee, composed of an equal number of members from each party, "formulate procedural rules...set up a timetable...determine the admissibility of evidence...decide what standard of proof should be required...(and) narrow the issues by screening the evidence."

Although a number of Democrats opposed the subcommittee idea, reluctant to delegate too much of the grand jury function of the committee in an impeachment inquiry, Ray Thornton (D Ark.), a freshman, backed the idea of a small bipartisan panel "to accept evidence and conduct hearings."

Creation of the advisory group by Rodino took the steam out of the drive for a select committee, although it could be revived since there was little indication that the advisory body would perform as anything more than a steering committee.

An Impeachable Offense? Ultimately, it would be for each member of the committee—and possibly the House—to decide the definition of an impeachable offense. That debate had begun with the Constitution, and recurred with each impeachment attempt. Traditionally, those more reluctant to see impeachment of the accused official defined an impeachable offense more narrowly than those who were supporting impeachment. Rodino agreed that the problem was "something we're going to have to reason with."

And practical reasons militated for a committee determination—at least of what was not likely to be an impeachable offense. Initially, the staff investigation was divided into the areas of President Nixon's personal finances, his campaign finances, Watergate, and possible abuse of presidential authority in matters such as impoundment and secret bombing.

In order not to waste Judiciary Committee staff time and energy, the committee should "decide what of the charges shows promise of being an impeachable offense," and then "give the rest" away to committees who might write legislation to prevent further such misconduct, Wiggins told Congressional Quarterly. He distinguished between a legally impeachable offense and a politically impeachable offense. Political popularity, he noted, can offset a technically impeachable offense: "There will be no votes to impeach a president if the people condone what he has done."

Expressing the need for some definition in a different—and more partisan—context, Lott advised: "What needs to be done is for the Democrats to draw a line and say, 'At least this much must be proved for us to go on to impeachment,' and for the Republicans to do the same, and say, 'If this much is proved, then we will have an impeachable offense.'"

The advisory group agreed Jan. 24 to hold open committee hearings in February on the definition of an impeachable offense. Doar said that that definition was one of the first matters for the committee to resolve.

Access to Information. Ironically, despite hours of investigation by all three branches of the government, and the news media, one of the problems facing the House Judiciary Committee was its access to information and evidence to confirm or refute the charges brought against Nixon.

Early in the inquiry, Rodino said the committee would look to other committees which already had inquired into some of these matters for their evidence. Chief among these was the Senate Watergate Committee. Doar said Jan. 7 that he had received no material yet from the committee but that he did have assurances that such was forthcoming.

"It is the desire and the political interest of the majority to not have rules, so that there can be the broadest possible range for the investigation. But the interest of the law and the minority are served by deciding the rules first."

—Charles E. Wiggins (R Calif.)

A major problem arose in mid-January, however, when special prosecutor Leon Jaworski, after at least two meetings with Doar, said that he would not make available to the Judiciary Committee the material he had received from the White House. All of that, he said, "we have insisted upon as part of our investigation, and when we received the material it was accompanied by the stated understanding that it was made available to us under an agreement of confidentiality."

Earlier that week White House Counsel J. Fred Buzhardt, terming the impeachment inquiry a basically political matter, had said that the White House would resist the committee's demands for presidential documents and tapes.

"The Committee on the Judiciary will have to seek subpoena power from the House" for the impeachment inquiry, Rodino announced Jan. 7. The purpose of this move was to perfect the committee's right to this power and so to ensure against any challenge of its subpoenas.

As granted to many standing committees by the Rules of the House, the power of subpoena generally was seen as intended for use in regard to matters within the committee's jurisdiction. As of January 1974, impeachment was not specifically included within the jurisdiction of the House Judiciary Committee, an omission which could raise questions about the propriety of its use of its usual subpoena power in regard to an impeachment inquiry. A clear grant of subpoena power from the House to the committee for this inquiry would scotch such questions.

This new subpoena matter raised questions on which partisan lines threatened to form again. The key, Railsback said Jan. 7, was whether Rodino would share this power. The answer came soon. The advisory group Jan. 24 agreed on a resolution by which the House granted this special power to the committee, to be exercised by Rodino and Hutchinson together, with any disagreements settled by the full committee.

Rodino said Jan. 24 that the committee had received a letter from Jaworski indicating a willingness to work out procedures for cooperation on evidence.

Outlook: Cloudy

"All of us...are aware," said Rodino Jan. 8, "that partisanship may crop up from time to time...but this (inquiry) must be conducted in a bipartisan manner." Hutchinson, a few days earlier, also had forecast the committee's working relationship during the inquiry in fairly optimistic terms: "I expect to see outcroppings of more partisanship in regard to impeachment than in regard to general legislative matters...but I know that every attempt will be made to keep political partisanship at its lowest level."

"It would, however, be unrealistic to expect this to be devoid of partisanship," he added.

More pessimistic forecasts were voiced by two other committee members. "I just can't see this turning out nonpartisan," says Flowers, whose hometown newspaper already had labeled him one of the "swing" votes on the matter. "But I hope it does," he added.

"It has all been decided," lamented Lott, one of the more conservative Republicans on the committee. "We are just going through an exercise. Right now I doubt whether it will be expeditious or fair.... All we can do is try to see that what is done is done fairly."

A more measured reaction came from Cohen: "It's easy now to say that everything should be done in a nonpartisan manner, but there are some tough questions down the road.... We are anxious to protect our part, our voice in the proceedings."

"So far," he continued, "the things which may have created negative feelings in this regard have not colored the entire process; they are not yet strong enough to skew it all."

PROFILES OF THE 38 JUDICIARY COMMITTEE MEMBERS

Following are profiles, in order of seniority, of all 38 members of the House Judiciary Committee—21 Democrats and 17 Republicans. Included are district descriptions, presidential support scores for 1973 and any comments each member may have made concerning the impeachment investigation.

THE DEMOCRATS

Peter W. Rodino Jr., 64, represents New Jersey's 10th district (Newark), which was in 1974 about 52 per cent black. A member of the House since 1949 and chairman of the committee since 1973, he faces the possibility of a strong primary challenge from a black candidate in 1974. A liberal, he supported Nixon on 28 per cent of the votes on which the President took a position during 1973. He has commented: "I must say that the consideration of resolutions relating to the possible impeachment of the President is a task I would have preferred not to undertake."

Harold D. Donohue, 72, represents Massachusetts' heavily industrialized 3rd district (central, Worcester). First elected to the House in 1947, Donohue did not go on the Judiciary Committee until the early 1950s, after Rodino. A quiet man who heads the Subcommittee on Claims, Donohue has a liberal voting record, supporting Nixon on 28 per cent of the votes in 1973.

Jack Brooks, 51, represents Texas' industrial 9th district (Beaumont-Port Arthur, Galveston). Brooks was first elected to the House in 1952 at the age of 29. He is a tough and outspoken liberal, was close to Lyndon Johnson and active on civil rights issues. He chairs the government operations subcommittee which investigated federal spending on the presidential homes at San Clemente, Calif., and Key Biscayne, Fla. He supported Nixon on 34 per cent of the votes in 1973.

Robert W. Kastenmeier, 49, represents Wisconsin's 2nd district, which includes the University of Wisconsin at Madison (southern). He has been a member of the House since 1959, is a highly regarded, issue-oriented liberal, and serves as chairman of the Subcommittee on Courts, Civil Liberties, and the Administration of Justice. He supported Nixon on 26 per cent of the votes in 1973. Kastenmeier has not said that he favors impeachment, but commented that before the "Saturday night massacre" firing of Archibald Cox, impeachment was "really unthinkable in practical terms. That is no longer the case."

Don Edwards, 58, represents the blue-collar suburbs of California's 9th district (Oakland to San Jose). He has been a member of the House since 1963, is a former FBI agent and national chairman of the Americans for Democratic Action. Edwards has gained the reputation of a hard-working liberal and is chairman of the Subcommittee on Civil Rights and Constitutional Rights. In 1973, he supported Nixon on 21 per cent of the votes. "We plan to prepare through our staff the most honest hard-hitting bill of particulars we can get," he has said, "and then present it to the American people."

William L. Hungate, 51, represents the rural and small-town 9th district of Missouri (northeast, St. Charles). A moderately liberal member of the House since 1964, Hungate heads the hard-working Subcommittee on Reform of Federal Criminal Laws. He supported Nixon on 34 per cent of the votes during 1973.

John Conyers Jr., 44, represents Michigan's predominantly black 1st district (residential areas of Detroit). A member of the House since 1966 and a forceful proponent of civil rights measures, Conyers heads the Subcommittee on Crime. He supported Nixon on 20 per cent of the votes during 1973.

Peter W. Rodino Jr.
(D N.J.)

Harold D. Donohue
(D Mass.)

Jack Brooks
(D Texas)

Robert W. Kastenmeier
(D Wis.)

Don Edwards
(D Calif.)

Joshua Eilberg, 52, represents Pennsylvania's middle-income residential 4th district (Philadelphia). He is a former majority leader in the state house of representatives, and was elected to the House in 1966. Liberal, quiet and hard-working, he heads the Subcommittee on Immigration, Citizenship, and International Law. He supported Nixon on 28 per cent of the votes in 1973. Eilberg has said that he would define an impeachable offense as a presidential action "which shocks the conscience," not necessarily a criminal action.

Jerome R. Waldie, 48, represents California's heavily industrial 14th district (most of Contra Costa County). Former majority leader of the state legislature, Waldie was elected to the House in 1966. He is regarded as very liberal and independent, and as one of the best lawyers on the committee. He is planning to run for governor of California in 1974. Waldie supported Nixon's position on 20 per cent of the votes during 1973. Sponsor of the first impeachment resolution introduced after the Cox firing, Waldie has said that "gross abuse of the office of the presidency, whether it is criminal or not, could be proper grounds for impeachment."

Walter Flowers, 40, represents the conservative Democratic 7th district of Alabama (west central, Tuscaloosa, Birmingham suburbs). He is a moderately conservative third-term member of the House, supporting Nixon's position 50 per cent of the time in 1973. Flowers has said that Congress has great latitude in defining an impeachable offense, but that it should not impeach a president simply because of "a lot of small things" or mere "distaste" for his actions.

James R. Mann, 53, represents the heavily industrialized 4th district of South Carolina (Greenville/Spartanburg). He is a former prosecutor, was elected to the House in 1969, and is regarded as one of the most conservative Democrats on the committee, supporting Nixon on 59 per cent of the votes in 1973. "Impeachment merely reveals the failure of the Judiciary Committee to exercise its oversight function" Mann has noted. "Congress is merely doing its duty to police executive power."

Paul S. Sarbanes, 40, represents the Baltimore suburbs of Maryland's 3rd district. Son of Greek immigrants, a Rhodes scholar and former state legislator, Sarbanes was elected to the House in 1970. He is a liberal with strong labor backing, and is respected by colleagues for his thoughtful intelligence. In 1973 he supported Nixon on 28 per cent of the votes.

John F. Seiberling, 55, represents Ohio's 14th district, which includes Akron and Kent State University. He is a decorated veteran of World War II, and was an attorney for the Goodyear Rubber Company—which his grandfather founded—before winning election to the House in 1970. Considered very liberal, he supported Nixon's position 25 per cent of the time in 1973.

George E. Danielson, 58, represents California's 29th district, which includes eastern Los Angeles. He is a former FBI agent and state legislator, and was elected to the House in 1970 with labor backing. Danielson has a tenuous hold on his seat because of recent redistricting, which placed him in the same district as Chet Holifield (D Calif.), chairman of the Government Operations

William L. Hungate
(D Mo.)

John Conyers Jr.
(D Mich.)

Joshua Eilberg
(D Pa.)

Jerome R. Waldie
(D Calif.)

Walter Flowers
(D Ala.)

| James R. Mann
(D S.C.) | Paul S. Sarbanes
(D Md.) | John F. Seiberling
(D Ohio) | George E. Danielson
(D Calif.) | Robert F. Drinan
(D Mass.) |

Committee. Danielson, a liberal, supported Nixon's position 22 per cent of the time in 1973. He has said that an impeachable offense should be defined narrowly as an indictable offense.

Robert F. Drinan, 53, represents Massachusetts' suburban and small-town 4th district (Boston suburbs, small industrial towns). Drinan is a Jesuit priest and former dean of Boston College Law School. He was elected to the House in 1970 and 1972 by narrow margins, has been highly critical of Nixon and was the first member of Congress (on July 31, 1973) to introduce an impeachment resolution. He has been a flamboyant spokesman for liberal causes, supporting Nixon on 33 per cent of the votes in 1973. "The first illusion we have to break is that you have to prove a criminal offense (to impeach the President). This is a political offense."

Charles B. Rangel, 43, represents New York's 19th district (Manhattan, Harlem). He is a former state legislator who defeated Adam Clayton Powell Jr. in a 1970 primary. In June 1973, he proposed that a special committee should be formed "to see if the President's role in the events surrounding the Watergate bugging and its subsequent coverup constituted grounds for impeachment." Rangel supported Nixon on 27 per cent of the votes in 1973.

Barbara C. Jordan, 36, represents Texas' primarily black 18th district (central Houston). She is a former state senator, was elected in 1972 as the first black woman to serve in Congress from the South and is an articulate and well respected member of the committee. She supported Nixon on 30 per cent of the votes in 1973.

Ray Thornton, 45, represents Arkansas' agricultural 4th district. A former state attorney general, he was elected to the House in 1972. He supported Nixon on 45 per cent of the votes in 1973 and has avoided making public statements concerning impeachment.

Elizabeth Holtzman, 32, represents New York's 16th district (Brooklyn) after upsetting former House dean and Judiciary Committee Chairman Emanuel Celler in the 1972 primary. She is a former state committeewoman, a liberal and is regarded as highly intelligent and hard-working. She supported Nixon's position 29 per cent of the time during 1973. She has commented: "We don't help to restore public confidence in the processes of government if we don't act expeditiously, with thoroughness, fairness and justice."

Wayne Owens, 36, represents Utah's 2nd district (Salt Lake City). A liberal who worked in the Robert F. Kennedy 1968 presidential primary campaign, Owens is expected to run for a Senate seat in 1974. He supported Nixon's position 32 per cent of the time in 1973.

Edward Mezvinsky, 36, was elected in 1972 over an incumbent Republican to represent Iowa's rural and rapidly growing industrial first district. He is a consumer advocate, a strong liberal, and a freshman spokesman in the House. He supported Nixon on 34 per cent of the votes in 1973.

| Charles B. Rangel
(D N.Y.) | Barbara C. Jordan
(D Texas) | Ray Thornton
(D Ark.) | Elizabeth Holtzman
(D N.Y.) | Wayne Owens
(D Utah) |

Edward Mezvinsky
(D Iowa)

Edward Hutchinson
(R Mich.)

Robert McClory
(R Ill.)

Henry P. Smith III
(R N.Y.)

Charles W. Sandman Jr.
(R N.J.)

THE REPUBLICANS

Edward Hutchinson, 59, represents Michigan's rural and small-town 4th district. He is a former state legislator who was elected to the House in 1963. He is conservative and quiet, preferring to stay out of the public eye. He supported Nixon's position 75 per cent of the time in 1973. "We've only got one president," he has said, "and impeachment of a president is something the country can't afford."

Robert McClory, 65, represents the outer Chicago suburbs of Illinois' 13th district. He has served in the House since 1963. Although he is of equal seniority as Hutchinson, he ranks second on the Republican side because of a draw for position. He has won reelection by wide margins in the past, but faces an energetic challenger for his seat in the March primary. He supported Nixon's position 67 per cent of the time in 1973. "There should be some kind of criminal offense (to justify impeachment)," he has said, "and there has to be direct evidence of (the President's) involvement."

Henry P. Smith III, 62, represents New York's 36th district (Niagara County). He is a conservative, elected to the House in 1964, and faces a strong Democratic challenger in 1974. In 1973, Smith supported Nixon on 68 per cent of the votes. He has not commented on impeachment.

Charles W. Sandman Jr., 52, represents the rural areas and resorts in the 2nd district of New Jersey. Former majority leader of the state senate and a member of the House since 1967, Sandman was soundly defeated in a 1973 race for governor. He is very conservative, supporting Nixon on 44 per cent of the votes in 1973. He missed a number of votes while campaigning for governor. He has said it is not proper for him as a member of the committee, to "prejudge" the impeachment case, and therefore has made no other public comment.

Tom Railsback, 41, represents Illinois' 19th district (western). He is a former state legislator and popular moderate conservative with labor support. He was first elected to the House in 1967 and is one of the more outspoken Republicans on the committee. He supported Nixon on 51 per cent of the votes in 1973. "You have an impeachment by the Democrats without any Republican participation," he has asserted, "and it's going to divide the country."

Charles E. Wiggins, 46, represents the primarily blue-collar suburbs of California's 25th district (eastern Los Angeles county), essentially the district Nixon once represented (1947-50). A thoughtful conservative considered by many the best legal mind on the committee, Wiggins was first elected to the House in 1967. He supported Nixon's position 64 per cent of the time in 1973. The President would be impeachable, he has said, for "conduct which, exposed to the light of day, produces moral outrage among the people that causes them to believe that he is no longer fit to serve."

David W. Dennis, 61, represents the industrial and agricultural 10th district of Indiana (Muncie and Richmond). Dennis is expected to face a tough fight for his seat in 1974. He supported Nixon on 76 per cent of the votes in 1973.

Tom Railsback
(R Ill.)

Charles E. Wiggins
(R Calif.)

David W. Dennis
(R Ind.)

Hamilton Fish Jr.
(R N.Y.)

Wiley Mayne
(R Iowa)

| Lawrence J. Hogan (R Md.) | M. Caldwell Butler (R Va.) | William S. Cohen (R Maine) | Trent Lott (R Miss.) | Harold V. Froehlich (R Wis.) |

Hamilton Fish Jr., 47, represents the Hudson River communities of New York's 25th district (outer New York City suburbs, farms and small industrial towns). A moderate Republican first elected to the House in 1968, Fish supported Nixon on 49 per cent of the votes in 1973. He has said that an impeachable offense is not necessarily an indictable offense.

Wiley Mayne, 56, represents Iowa's agricultural 6th district (northwest). Elected to the House in 1966, he won with only 52 per cent of the vote in 1972, and is likely to face a strong challenge in the 1974 election. He supported Nixon on 70 per cent of the votes in 1973. Mayne feels that an impeachable offense must be a crime.

Lawrence J. Hogan, 45, represents the Washington, D.C., suburbs of Maryland's 5th district. A former FBI agent, elected to the House in 1968, Hogan is a strong conservative and supported Nixon on 67 per cent of the votes in 1973. He has stated: "We ought to disqualify those members from the grand jury (the House Judiciary Committee considering impeachment charges) who have said that the President ought to be impeached."

M. Caldwell Butler, 48, represents the traditionally Republican 6th district of Virginia (western, Roanoke). He is a former Republican leader in the state assembly and campaign manager for former Rep. Richard H. Poff (R 1952-72), who also was a Judiciary Committee member. Butler was elected in 1972 to fill Poff's seat. He supported Nixon's position 75 per cent of the time in 1973. "The time has come to impeach or ceasefire," he has said.

William S. Cohen, 33, represents Maine's 2nd district, which includes Bangor, a city of which he was formerly mayor. Elected in 1972 to his first House term after a walking campaign, he has been mentioned as a possible gubernatorial candidate. Cohen supported Nixon on 53 per cent of the votes in 1973. In defining an impeachable offense, he has said: "It's like Robert Frost on love. It's indefinable and unmistakable—I know it when I see it."

Trent Lott, 32, represents the rapidly growing resort and industrial areas of Mississippi's 5th district (southeast). Formerly administrative assistant to now-retired Rep. William M. Colmer (D Miss. 1933-1973), Lott became a Republican and won Colmer's seat in 1972. A very conservative member, he supported Nixon's position 69 per cent of the time in 1973.

Harold V. Froehlich, 41, represents Wisconsin's rural 8th district (northeast). He was elected to the House by a narrow margin in 1972 and faces a hard contest in 1974 to hold his seat. He supported Nixon's position 60 per cent of the time in 1973.

Carlos J. Moorhead, 51, represents the conservative white-collar 20th district of California (Los Angeles). A former state assemblyman, he supported Nixon on 70 per cent of the votes during 1973. Impeachment should only come for criminal acts, he maintains. "The President has done a remarkable job considering Congress has spent $1-million to try to impeach him."

Joseph J. Maraziti, 61, represents the new rural 13th district in New Jersey (west). He is a former judge and state legislator. A moderate, he supported Nixon's position 61 per cent of the time in 1973.

Delbert L. Latta, 53, represents the largely agricultural 5th district of Ohio (northwest). Latta, a veteran Republican legislator, was first elected to the House in 1958. A conservative, Latta supported President Nixon's position 72 per cent of the time in 1973. Latta says "all impeachment proceedings must be defined within the confines of the Constitution, nothing more, nothing less."

| Carlos J. Moorhead (R Calif.) | Joseph J. Maraziti (R N.J.) | Delbert L. Latta (R Ohio) |

CONTRIBUTIONS TO HOUSE JUDICIARY COMMITTEE MEMBERS

The 38 members of the House Judiciary Committee received a total of $680,460 in donations during the 1972 campaign from organizations contributing over $100, according to figures compiled by Common Cause. The 21 Democratic members received $352,647, while the 17 Republican members collected $327,613.

Nearly half of the contributions to Democratic representatives came from organized labor ($161,475), which was not a major source for the Republicans ($1,550). The bulk of labor contributions to Democratic committee members came from the AFL-CIO and its affiliated unions. Thirty-eight unions, two departments and the AFL-CIO's Committee on Political Education (COPE) contributed a combined total of $134,324 to the Democratic members of the committee.

The largest contribution went to Chairman Peter W. Rodino Jr. (D N.J.), who received $24,100 from the AFL-CIO. COPE alone contributed $13,000. In all, Rodino received $44,300 in campaign contributions from 46 different organizations, 25 of them labor unions.

Republican committee members received over half their 1972 contributions from Republican Party organizations ($200,167) at the national, state and local levels. Other major sources of support were state branches of the American Medical Association (AMA), $45,500, and the National Association of Manufacturers Business-Industry Political Action Committee (BIPAC), $22,000. The AMA affiliates contributed $10,000 each to the 1972 campaigns of Representatives David W. Dennis (R Ind.) and Carlos J. Moorhead (R Calif.) and amounts ranging from $500 to $5,500 to 11 other Republican members. BIPAC made contributions ranging from $1,000 to $4,000 to 11 Republican members.

Rep. Edward Hutchinson (Mich.), the ranking Republican member of the committee, received $6,200 in campaign donations from seven organizations. Four of the organizations, giving a total of $4,000, were affiliated with the Republican Party. The other contributions came from the Michigan Doctors Political Action Committee (Michigan branch, AMA), $1,000; the Associated General Contractors Committee for Action, $1,000; and the National Association of Life Underwriters Political Action Committee, $200.

The leading recipients of contributions among Judiciary Committee members were Wayne Owens (D Utah), $53,739; Edward Mezvinsky (D Iowa), $52,070; and Harold V. Froehlich (R Wis.), $50,395.

Following is a complete list of campaign contributions of over $100 made by organizations during the 1972 campaign to members of the committee.

Democrats

Peter W. Rodino Jr. (N.J.), chairman, $44,300: AFL-CIO Committee on Political Education (COPE), $13,000; AFL-CIO Industrial Union Department, $1,000; Amalgamated Clothing Workers Political Education Committee (AFL-CIO), $300; Amal-

gamated Meat Cutters and Butcher Workers of North America (AFL-CIO), $100; American Dairymen's Political Education, Mid America Dairymen (ADEPT), $2,000; American Federation of Musicians (AFL-CIO), $250; American Federation of State, County and Municipal Employees National People Commitee (AFL-CIO), $200; American Hotel and Motel Political Action Committee (AHMPAC), $300; Bankers Political Action Committee (BANKPAC), Washington area, $200; Carpenters Legislative Improvement Committee (AFL-CIO), $700; Certified Shorthand Reporters Association of New Jersey, $500; Committee of Automotive Retailers, $300; Committee for Thorough Agricultural Political Education (Associated Milk Producers, Inc.), $1,000; Communications Workers of America (AFL-CIO), $500; Democratic Congressional Campaign Committee, $6,700; DRIVE Political Fund (Teamsters), $1,000; Engineers Political Education Committee (AFL-CIO), $200; Gas Employees Political Election Committee, $200; Hotel, Restaurant Employees and Bartenders International Union (AFL-CIO), $250; International Association of Fire Fighters Committee on Political Education (AFL-CIO), $300; International Association of Machinists, District 47 (AFL-CIO), $1,000; International Brotherhood of Electrical Workers (AFL-CIO), $500; International Ladies Garment Workers Union (ILGWU), Eastern Region Campaign Committee (AFL-CIO), $500; Johnson and Johnson Employees Good Government Fund, $500; Machinists Non-Partisan Political League (AFL-CIO), $200; Maintenance of Way Political League (AFL-CIO), $300; Mortgage Bankers Political Action Committee (MORPAC), $200; National Association of Life Underwriters Political Action Committee, $200; National Cable TV Association (PACT), $1,200; New Jersey State Carpenters Non-Partisan Political Committee, $1,000; Railway Clerks Political League (AFL-CIO), $500; Railway Labor Executives Association Political League (AFL-CIO), $200; Real Estate Political Education Committee of New Jersey, $500; Recording Artists Political Action Committee, $300; Retail Clerks International Association, Active Ballot Club (AFL-CIO), $500; Retail Store Employees Union, Active Ballot Club, Local 1262 (AFL-CIO), $250; Seafarers Political Activity Donation (AFL-CIO), $1,500; Service Employees International Union Committee on Political Education (AFL-CIO), $200; Smith, Klein and French Voluntary Non-Partisan Political Fund, $150; Special Political Agricultural Community Education (SPACE Dairymen Inc.), $1,000; Textile Workers Union AFL-CIO, $750; Tobacco Peoples Public Affairs Committee, $200; Transportation Political Education League (United Transportation Union, AFL-CIO), $500; Truck Operators Non-Partisan Committee, $1,000; United Automobile Workers (UAW) Voluntary Community Action Program, Region 9, $750; United Steelworkers Political Action Fund (AFL-CIO), $500.

Harold O. Donohue (Mass.), $1,500: Amalgamated Meat Cutters and Butchers of North America (AFL-CIO), $300; American Insurance Men's Political Action Committee, $200; Democratic Congressional Campaign Committee, $1,000.

Jack Brooks (Texas), $22,950: Amalgamated Meat Cutters and Butchers (AFL-CIO), $300; Carpenters Legislative Improvement Committee (AFL-CIO), $500; Democratic Congressional Campaign Committee, $9,900; Engineers Political Education Committee (AFL-CIO), $250; National Maritime Union Fighting Fund, $500; National Rural Electric Cooperative Association Action Committee for Rural Electrification, $500; Political Committee for Design Professionals, $10,000; Seafarers Political Activity Donation (AFL-CIO),

$300; Transportation Political Education League (AFL-CIO), $500; UAW Voluntary Community Action Program, $200.

Robert W. Kastenmeier (Wis.), $14,642: Amalgamated Clothing Workers, Midwest Regional Joint Board Political Education Committee (AFL-CIO), $200; Amalgamated Meat Cutters and Butchers of America (AFL-CIO), $300; Carpenters Legislative Improvement Committee (AFL-CIO), $500; Committee for Thorough Agricultural Political Education, $2,650; Communications Workers of America (AFL-CIO), $600; D.C. Friends of Kastenmeier Committee, $624; Democratic Congressional Campaign Committee, $500; Democratic Party of Green County, $410; Democratic Party of Iowa County, $250; DRIVE Local 695 (Teamsters), $200; Machinists Non-Partisan Political League (AFL-CIO), $1,000; National Council of Farmer Cooperatives (PACE), $250; National Rural Electric Cooperative Association Action Committee for Rural Electrification, $500; National Rural Electric Cooperative Association, Wisconsin Action Committee for Rural Electrification, $200; Retail Clerks Active Ballot Club (AFL-CIO), $450; Sheet Metal Workers Political Action League (AFL-CIO), $500; Textile Workers Political Fund, $250; Transportation Political Education League (AFL-CIO), $500; UAW Voluntary Community Action Program, $500; United Steelworkers Political Action Fund (AFL-CIO), $1,500; Vote for Peace, $758; Wisconsin AFL-CIO COPE, $2,000.

Don Edwards (Calif.), $10,302: AFL-CIO COPE, $1,500; California National Nominees Fund, $500; United Brotherhood of Carpenters and Joiners Local 316 (AFL-CIO), $200; Democratic Congressional Campaign Committee, $3,055; Laborers Political League (AFL-CIO), $500; Machinists Non-Partisan League, District Local 93 (AFL-CIO), $200; Retail Clerks International Association, Local 428, Active Ballot Club (AFL-CIO), $450; Transportation Political Education League (AFL-CIO), $600; UAW Voluntary Community Action Program, $300; United Democratic Finance Committee, $740; United Steelworkers Political Action Fund, $1,000; Vote for Peace, $757; Wells Fargo Bank, Good Government Committee, $500.

William L. Hungate (Mo.), $11,490: Agriculture and Dairy Education Political Trust (American Dairymen, Inc.), $1,000; Amalgamated Meat Cutters and Butchers (AFL-CIO), $300; American Dairy Association Political Trust Fund, $300; Associated Dairymen (Associated Milk Producers, Inc.), $1000; Communications Workers of America (AFL-CIO), $250; Democratic Congressional Campaign Committee, $4,000; Democratic Study Group Campaign Fund, $1,000; DRIVE Political Fund, Joint Council 13 (Teamsters), $250; Hannibal Trades and Labor Council, $200; ILGWU Political Trust Fund (AFL-CIO), $140; Laborers Political League (AFL-CIO), $500; Machinists Non-Partisan League (AFL-CIO), $500; National Association of Life Underwriters Political Action Committee, $250; National Cable TV Association, $250; Retail Store Employees (AFL-CIO), $250; Seafarers Political Activity Donation (AFL-CIO), $300; UAW, Region 5, $500; United Steelworkers, St. Louis Political Action Committee (AFL-CIO), $500.

John Conyers Jr. (Mich.), $7,850: AFL-CIO, Metropolitan Detroit Council, $820; Democratic Congressional Campaign Committee, $250; DRIVE Political Fund (Teamsters), $1,000; Engineers Political Education Committee (AFL-CIO), $250; Laborers Political Action League (AFL-CIO), $500; National Rural Electric Cooperative Association, Action Committee for Rural Electrification, $300; Maintenance of Way Political League (AFL-CIO), $500; Transportation Political Education League (AFL-CIO), $300; United Automobile, Aerospace, and Agricultural Workers, Committee for Good Government, $200; UAW Voluntary Community Action Program, $685; Vote for Peace, $1795; Women in Community Service, $1,250.

Joshua Eilberg (Pa.), $20,150: AFL-CIO COPE, $2,500; Amalgamated Clothing Workers Political Education Committee of Philadelphia (AFL-CIO), $500; Amalgamated Meat Cutters and Butchers (AFL-CIO), $300; Building and Construction Trades Department, Political Education Fund (AFL-CIO), $500; Carpenters Legislative Improvement Committee (AFL-CIO),

$700; D.C. Committee of Businessmen to Assist Congressional Candidates, $500; Democratic Congressional Campaign Committee, $2,500; Firemen and Oilers Political League (AFL-CIO), $200; Fraternal Order of Police, Philadelphia Lodge #5, $200; International Brotherhood of Electrical Workers (AFL-CIO), $200; International Brotherhood of Printers and Allied Trades (AFL-CIO), $200; International Brotherhood of Pulp Sulphite and Paper Mill Workers (AFL-CIO), $1,000; ILGWU (AFL-CIO), $500; ILGWU, Knitgoods Local 190 (AFL-CIO), $500; Knitgoods Legislative Education Fund, $200; Labors' League for Political Education, Electrical Branch #98, $700; Laborers' Political Action League (AFL-CIO), $500; Machinists Non-Partisan Political League (AFL-CIO), $500; Maintenance of Way Political League (AFL-CIO), $500; National Life Underwriters Political Action Committee, $200; National Rural Electric Cooperative Association Action Committee for Rural Electrification, $250; Philadelphia Police, Fire and Park Police Federal Credit Union, $400; Railway Clerks Political League (AFL-CIO), $1,500; Retail Clerks International Association, Active Ballot Club (AFL-CIO), $250; Savings Association Public Affairs Committee, $300; Seafarers Political Activity Donation (AFL-CIO), $1,000; Sheet Metal Workers League for Political Education (AFL-CIO), $500; Shipwright Joiners, Local 1856, $200; Steam Fitters Union, Local 420, $500; Transportation Political Education League (AFL-CIO), $600; UAW, $500; United Brotherhood of Carpenters and Joiners (AFL-CIO), $250; United Steelworkers Political Action Committee Fund (AFL-CIO), $1,000.

Jerome R. Waldie (Calif.), $12,898: Alameda-Contra Costa Medical Association, $300; Amalgamated Meat Cutters and Butchers (AFL-CIO), $250; California Democratic National Nominees Fund, $500; California Medical Political Action Committee (California branch, American Medical Association), $1,000; Carpenters Legislative Improvement Committee (AFL-CIO), $800; Del Monte Corporation Voluntary Non-Partisan Good Government Fund, $300; Democratic Congressional Campaign Committee, $3,055; General Telephone Employees Good Government Club, $300; International Association of Fire Fighters (AFL-CIO), $500; International Union of Operating Engravers Voluntary Political Fund (AFL-CIO), $500; Laborers' Political League (AFL-CIO), $500; National Association of Life Underwriters Political Action Committee, $200; National Maritime Union Fighting Fund, $500; Transportation Political Education League (AFL-CIO), $200; UAW Voluntary Community Action Program, $500; United Democratic Finance Committee, $678; United Steelworkers of America Political Action Fund (AFL-CIO), $500; United Transportation Union, $300; Vote for Peace, $1,515; Wells Fargo Bank, Good Government Committee, $500.

Walter Flowers (Ala.), $5,249: Alabama Medical Association Political Action Committee, $3,000; Alabama Realtors Association, $500; Governors Committee to Elect Democrats, $1,749.

James R. Mann (S. C.), $4,625: Committee of 100 (Democratic Party organization), $500; Democratic Congressional Campaign Committee, $2,000; Democratic Party of Greenville County, $325; Savings Association Political Affairs Committee, $300; South Carolina Electric Co-operative Association, $500; South Carolina Political Action Committee, $1,000.

Paul S. Sarbanes (Md.), $10,125: AFL-CIO COPE, $2,300; Amalgamated Clothing Workers of America Political Education Committee, Baltimore Region Joint Board (AFL-CIO), $500; American Federation of State, County and Municipal Employees National People Committee (AFL-CIO), $1,000; Coolahan-Malene Committee, $250; Democratic Congressional Campaign Committee, $500; DRIVE Political Fund (Teamsters), Joint Council 62, $1,000; Laborers Political Action League (AFL-CIO), $500; National Maritime Union Fighting Fund, $250; Retail Clerks International Association, Active Ballot Club, Local 692, $1,250; Seafarers Political Activity Donation (AFL-CIO), $1,000; Transportation Political Education League (AFL-CIO), $300; UAW Voluntary Community Action Program, $1,275.

John F. Seiberling (Ohio), $11,400: AFL-CIO COPE, $2,000; Amalgamated Meat Cutters and Butchers (AFL-CIO), $400; American Federation of State, County and Municipal Employees,

National People Committee (AFL-CIO), $500; Communication Workers of America (AFL-CIO), $300; Democratic Congressional Campaign Committee, $500; Democratic Study Group Campaign Committee, $1,000; Hotel and Restaurant Employees and Bartenders International Union, Committee on Political Education (AFL-CIO), $250; International Brotherhood of Electrical Workers (AFL-CIO), $500; International Chemical Workers Union Voluntary Live Fund, $500; ILGWU Campaign Committee (AFL-CIO), $250; Laborer's Political League (AFL-CIO), $500; Machinists Non-Partisan Political League (AFL-CIO), $500; Ohio DRIVE Local, $200; Sheet Metal Workers' International Association Political Action League (AFL-CIO), $500; UAW Voluntary Community Action Program, $2,000; United Rubber Cork, Linoleum and Plastic Workers (AFL-CIO), $500; United Steelworkers, Akron Political Fund (AFL-CIO), $1,000.

George E. Danielson (Calif.), $11,097: AFL-CIO COPE, Los Angeles, $250; Amalgamated Meat Cutters and Butchers (AFL-CIO), $300; Democratic Congressional Campaign Committee, $5,305; Democratic State Central Committee of California, $642; Electrical Workers Political Education Committee (AFL-CIO), $300; General Telephone Employees Good Government Club, $800; Hotel and Restaurant Employees and Bartenders International Union (AFL-CIO), $300; Laborers' Political League (AFL-CIO), $1,000; Machinists Non-Partisan Political League (AFL-CIO), $500; Transportation Political Education League (AFL-CIO), $900; UAW Voluntary Community Action Program, $300; United Steelworkers Political Action Fund (AFL-CIO), $500.

Robert F. Drinan (Mass.), $20,314: AFL-CIO COPE, $3,000; AFL-CIO Industrial Union Department Voluntary Funds, $500; Amalgamated Clothing Workers, Boston (AFL-CIO), $300; Amalgamated Meat Cutters and Butchers (AFL-CIO), $300; American Federation of State, County and Municipal Employees (AFL-CIO), $250; Communications Workers of America (AFL-CIO), $300; Democratic Congressional Campaign Committee, $6,000; Democratic Study Group Campaign Fund, $2,000; International Brotherhood of Electrical Workers (AFL-CIO), $200; ILGWU Campaign Committee (AFL-CIO), $250; International Union of Electrical Workers (AFL-CIO), $1,000; Machinists Non-Partisan Political League (AFL-CIO), $1,000; National Committee for an Effective Congress, $1,000; O'Neill for Congress and the Election of All Democratic Candidates Committee, $500; Railway Labor Executives Association Political League (AFL-CIO), $200; Retail Clerks International Association, Active Ballot Club (AFL-CIO), $500; Sheet Metal Workers (AFL-CIO), $200; Transportation Political Education League (AFL-CIO), $300; UAW Voluntary Community Action Program, $1,000; Vote for Peace, $1,514.

Charles B. Rangel (N.Y.), $3,593: (American Federation of State, County, and Municipal Employees) Council 37, $243; Amalgamated Clothing Workers (AFL-CIO), $300; Brotherhood of Railway, Airline and Steamship Clerks (AFL-CIO), $200; Chefs, Cooks, Pastry Cooks and Assistants Union of New York, Local 89, $200; Laborers' Political League (AFL-CIO), $500; New York Republican County Committee, $500; Railway Labor Executives Association Political League (AFL-CIO), $200; Savings Association League of New York, $200; Seafarers Political Activity Donation (AFL-CIO), $1,000; UAW Local 259, $250.

Barbara C. Jordan (Texas), $26,676: Amalgamated Meat Cutters and Butchers (AFL-CIO), $300; Amalgamated Clothing Workers (AFL-CIO), $300; American Federation of State, County and Municipal Employees, National People Committee (AFL-CIO), $500; Citizens for Good Government, $500; Committee on Voter Education, $1,502; Democratic Congressional Campaign Committee, $1,000; Democratic Study Group Campaign Fund, $1,000; DRIVE Fund (Teamsters), Local 745, $2,000; Engineers Political Education Committee (AFL-CIO), $250; Fire Fighters Committee on Political Education (AFL-CIO), $200; Friends of Barbara Jordan, $500; Friends of Barbara Jordan Committee,

$2,980; Friends of Jordan for Congress Committee, $500; Houston Apartment Owners Association, $1,000; Houston Barristers Wives, $130; Houston Voters Association, $300; International Brotherhood of Electrical Workers (AFL-CIO), $200; ILGWU (AFL-CIO), $250; International Longshoremens Association, Local 872 (AFL-CIO), $331; Laborers Political Action Committee (AFL-CIO), $300; Lawyers Involved for Texas, $500; Machinists Non-Partisan Political League (AFL-CIO), $500; Ministers Wives Charity Union, $300; Ministers Wives Social Club, $500; National Education Association Political Action Committee, $500; Oil, Chemical and Atomic Workers (AFL-CIO), $200; Seafarers Political Activity Donation (AFL-CIO), $500; Southern Texas Communications Workers of America (AFL-CIO), $500; Texas AFL-CIO, $3,000; Texas DRIVE Fund (Teamsters), $3,500; TEXPAC (Texas branch, American Medical Association), $1,000; Texas State Beauty Culture League #47, $206; UAW Committee on Political Education, $750; West End Civic Club, $177; Volunteers for Hatcher, $500.

Ray Thornton (Ark.), $3,400: AFL-CIO COPE, $1,000; Business-Industry Political Action Committee (BIPAC, affiliated with National Association of Manufacturers), $1,000; Machinists Non-Partisan Political League (AFL-CIO), $500; UAW, $400; United Steelworkers of America (AFL-CIO), $500.

Elizabeth Holtzman (N.Y.), $4,765: Amalgamated Clothing Workers (AFL-CIO), $250; Committee for Judge Nanette Dembitz, $500; Democratic Congressional Campaign Fund, $1,500; Democratic Study Group Campaign Fund, $1,000; Vote for Peace, $1,515.

Wayne Owens (Utah), $53,739: AFL-CIO COPE, $3,100; AFL-CIO Industrial Union Department, $2,000; Agriculture and Dairy Education Political Trust (Dairymen, Inc.), $1,000; Amalgamated Meat Cutters and Butchers (AFL-CIO), $500; Amalgamated Clothing Workers (AFL-CIO), $450; American Federation of State, County and Municipal Employees, National People Committee (AFL-CIO), $250; American Federation of Teachers, Million Dollar Fund (AFL-CIO), $200; Carpenters Legislative Improvement Committee (AFL-CIO), $1,000; Christmas Tree Center, $690; Committee for Thorough Agricultural Political Education (Associated Milk Producers Inc.), $1,600; Committee for Twelve, $4,400; Communications Workers of America (AFL-CIO), $1,300; Democratic Congressional Campaign Committee, $7,000; Democratic State Committee, $528; Democratic Study Group Campaign Fund, $3,000; DRIVE Fund (Teamsters), $2,550; Fire Fighters Committee on Political Education (AFL-CIO), $300; Firemen and Oilers Political League (AFL-CIO), $200; International Brotherhood of Electrical Workers (AFL-CIO), $550; ILGWU Campaign Committee (AFL-CIO), $400; International Union of Electrical, Radio and Machine Workers (AFL-CIO), $500; Laborers Political League (AFL-CIO), $800; League of Conservation Voters, $3,000; Machinists Non-Partisan Political League (AFL-CIO), $450; National Committee for an Effective Congress, $3,200; National Education Association Political Action Committee, $1,000; National Maritime Union Fighting Fund (AFL-CIO), $500; National Rural Electric Cooperative Association Action Committee for Rural Electrification, $800; Oil, Chemical and Atomic Workers Union Political Education Account (AFL-CIO), $500; Railway Clerks Political League (AFL-CIO), $300; Research Industries Corporation, $210; Seafarers Political Activity Donation (AFL-CIO), $300; Sheet Metal Workers International Association Political Action League (AFL-CIO), $500; Textile Workers Union Political Fund (AFL-CIO), $250; Transportation Political Education League (AFL-CIO), $690; Union Pacific Railroad Fund for Effective Government, $200; UAW Political Fund, $1,016; United Rubber, Cork, Linoleum and Plastic Workers (AFL-CIO), $300; United Steelworkers Political Action Fund (AFL-CIO), $3,500; University of Utah, $500; Utah Council for Improvement of Education, $3,500; Utah Dental Political Action Committee (Utah branch, American Dental Association), $200; Utah Motor Transport Association, $505.

Edward Mezvinsky (Iowa), $52,070: AFL-CIO COPE, $6,000; AFL-CIO Industrial Union Department, $500; Agriculture and Dairy Education Political Trust, $2,000; Amalgamated Meat Cutters and Butchers (AFL-CIO), $1,000; Amalgamated Clothing Workers (AFL-CIO), $250; American Federation of State, County and Municipal Employees, National People Committee (AFL-CIO), $250; American Federation of Teachers, Million Dollar Fund (AFL-CIO), $150; Bricklayers Action Committee (AFL-CIO), $250; Brooklyn Longshoremen's Political Action and Education Fund, $500; Building Trades Department, AFL-CIO, $250; Chicago Joint Board Political Education Fund, $200; Committee for Thorough Agricultural Political Education, $1,000; Communications Workers of America (AFL-CIO), $500; Dairy Farmers Political League (ADEPT), $4,000; Democratic Campaign Committee, First District, $6,670; Democratic Central Committee of Johnson County, $200; Democratic Congressional Campaign Committee, $8,500; Democratic National Congressional Committee, $1,500; Democratic State Committee, $500; Democratic Study Group Campaign Fund, $3,000; Democratic Womens Club of North Lee County, $200; DRIVE Fund, $2,500; International Brotherhood of Electrical Workers (AFL-CIO), $400; International Brotherhood of Painters and Allied Trades (AFL-CIO), $150; International Brotherhood of Pulp, Sulphite and Paper Mill Workers (AFL-CIO), $500; ILGWU (AFL-CIO), $800; International Union of Operating Engineers (AFL-CIO), $250; Lithographers and Photoengravers Union, $200; Machinists Non-Partisan Political League (AFL-CIO), $1,500; National Committee for an Effective Congress, $1,000; National Rural Electric Cooperative Association Action Committee for Rural Electrification, $500; Oil, Chemical and Atomic Workers Union (AFL-CIO), $300; Railway Clerks Political League (AFL-CIO), $500; Retail Clerks International Association, Active Ballot Club (AFL-CIO), $250; Sheet Metal Workers Political Action League (AFL-CIO), $250; Special Political Agricultural Community Education (SPACE), $2,500; Transport Workers Union Political Fund (AFL-CIO), $250; Transportation Political Education League (AFL-CIO), $500; UAW Voluntary Community Action Program, $2,000; United Rubber, Cork, Linoleum and Plastic Workers (AFL-CIO), $300.

Republicans

Edward Hutchinson (Mich.), $6,200: Associated General Contractors Committee for Action, $1,000; Michigan Doctors Political Action Committee (Michigan branch, AMA), $1,000; National Association of Life Underwriters Political Action Committee, $200; National Republican Congressional Committee, $2,000; Republican Committee of Coloma, $300; Republican Committee of Lenawee County, $500; Three Hundred Club of Republican Party of Michigan, Hillsdale County Chapter, $1,200.

Robert McClory (Ill.), $4,394: AMSCO-Union 76 Political Awareness Fund, $300; Anderson for Congress Finance Committee, $329; Committee for Thorough Agricultural Political Education (Associated Milk Producers, Inc.), $500; Fox Valley Sheet Metal Employers Committee, $265; National Republican Congressional Committee, $1,000; United Republican Fund, $2,000.

Henry P. Smith III (N.Y.), $28,275: Donations from some Bell Aerospace Co. employees, $1,000; BIPAC (affiliated with NAM), $2,000; Congressional Victory Committee, $1,000; D.C. Businessmen, $500; Empire Dental Political Action Committee (New York branch, American Dental Association), $200; Food Processors Public Affairs Committee, $250; Frontier Republican Women's Committee, $300; Kushner and Kushner, attorneys, $250; National Association of Life Underwriters Political Action Committee, $250; New York Republican Congressional Campaign Committee, $2,500; Republican Committee of Niagara County, $4,000; Republican National Committee, $14,375; Republican Twelve Committee, $1,500; SeniorMeadows of Niagara, $150.

Charles W. Sandman Jr. (N.J.), $6,500: BIPAC, $2,000; JEMPAC (New Jersey branch, AMA), $1,000; Johnson and Johnson Good Government Fund, $500; National Republican Campaign Committee, $3,000.

Tom Railsback (Ill.), $5,388: Committee for Thorough Agricultural Political Education, $500; Kemper Campaign Fund,

$250; National Council of Farmer Cooperatives, Political Action for Cooperative Effectiveness, $250; National Republican Congressional Committee, $1,450; Republican National Committee, $138; Transportation Political Education League (AFL-CIO), $300; UAW Voluntary Community Action Program, $500; United Republican Fund of Illinois, $2,000.

Charles E. Wiggins (Calif.), $13,565: BIPAC, $2,000; California Medical Political Committee and AMPAC (California branch, AMA), $3,500; General Telephone and Electronics Good Government Club, $250; Hacienda Heights Women's Club, $120; Hughes Aircraft Company Active Citizenship Fund, $720; Lincoln Club of Orange County, $1,000; National Association of Life Underwriters Political Action Committee, $250; National Association of Real Estate Boards Political Action Committee, $500; National Republican Congressional Committee, $2,000; Orange County Finance Committee, $825; Republican Women's Club of Rancho La Habra, $200; Republican Women's Club of Whittier, $200; Union Oil Bipartisan Political Fund, $500; Wells Fargo Bank Good Government Committee, $500; Whittier Lincoln Club, $1,000.

David W. Dennis (Ind.), $27,100: American Conservative Union, $1,000; BIPAC, $3,000; Friends of Rural Electrification, $500; IMPAC (Indiana branch, AMA), $10,000; Indiana Republican State Central Committee, $1,000; Lincolnia Club of Jay County, $700; National Association of Life Underwriters Political Action Committee, $200; National Association of Real Estate Boards Political Action Committee, $500; National Republican Congressional Committee, $7,000; Republican Central Committee of Hancock County, $500; Republican Twelve, $1,750; Republican Committee of Union City, $500; Union Oil Company Political Awareness Fund, $300; Young America's Campaign Committee (Young Americans for Freedom), $150.

Hamilton Fish Jr. (N.Y.), $5,425: American Dental Association Political Action Committee, $500; National Association of Life Underwriters Political Action Committee, $300; National Republican Congressional Committee, $2,000; New York Republican Congressional Campaign Committee, $2,500; Republican Committee, Town of Washington, $125.

Wiley Mayne (Iowa), $14,377: BIPAC, $1,000; Dickinson County Central Committee, $400; Iowa Medical Political Action Committee (Iowa branch, AMA), $500; National Committee for Support of Free Broadcasting, $250; National Confectioners Association Government Improvement Group, $300; National Republican Congressional Committee, $3,700; National Rural Electric Cooperative Association Action Committee for Rural Electrification, $500; PACE (AFL-CIO), $250; Plymouth County Central Committee, $500; Republican Central Committee, Clay County, $943; Republican Central Committee, Humboldt County, $300; Republican Central Committee, Winnebago County, $884; Republican Finance Committee, Monona, $350; Republican Party of Iowa Fed. Elections Account, $900; Republican Party of Plymouth County, $800; Republican State Central Committee, $2,000; Republican Women, Buena Vista County, $150; Republican Women, Sixth District Federation, $650.

Lawrence J. Hogan (Md.), $14,949: American Apparel Manufacturers Association Committee for American Principles, $500; BIPAC, $1,000; D.C. Republican Committee, $1,000; Elephant Club of Prince Georges County, $1,340; Government Improvement Group in Maryland, $400; International Association of Fire Fighters Committee on Political Education (AFL-CIO), $500; Maryland Medical Political Action Committee (Maryland branch, AMA), $2,000; National Association of Real Estate Boards Political Education Committee, $700; National Republican Congressional Committee, $2,000; Neighbor to Neighbor Drive, Prince Georges County, $609; Republican Central Committee for Prince Georges County, $250; Republican Women's Club, Bethesda, $200; Republican Women's Club, Bowie, $200; Republican Women's Club, Rock Creek, $500; Republican Women's Club, University Park, $300; Salute to Ted Agnew Night Committee, $2,500; Truck Operators Non-Partisan Committee, $500; Young Republican Club, Prince Georges County, $450.

M. Caldwell Butler (Va.), $32,950: American Medical Association Political Action Committee (AMPAC), $3,000; BIPAC, $1,000; Butler-Robinson Dinner Committee, $869; Committee to Re-elect the President, $3,000; Dentists for Butler, $900; National Republican Congressional Committee, $500; Physicians for Butler, $1,000; Republican City Committee, Lynchburg, $1,293; Republican City Committee, Roanoke, $900; Republican City Committee, Waynesboro, $1,000; Republican Committee, Botecourt County, $900; Republican Committee, Radford, $200; Republican Committee, Sixth District, $1,060; Republican Committee, Waynesboro, $800; Republican Congressional Boosters, $10,000; Republican Party, Bath County, $250; Republican Women's Club, Roanoke, $168; Republican Women's Club, Roanoke Valley, $280; Sixth District Farmers for Butler, $330; SPACE Virginia Trust (Dairymen, Inc.), $1,000; VAMPAC (Virginia branch, AMA), $4,000; Virginia Licensing Home Association (VANHEPAC), $500.

William S. Cohen (Maine), $33,700: American Dental Association Political Action Committee, $500; BIPAC, $4,000; Maine Medical Political Action Committee (Maine branch, AMA), $4,000; Maine Republican Finance Committee, $14,000; National Republican Congressional Committee, $5,200; Republican Committee, Oxford County, $200; Republican Congressional Boosters Club, $5,000; Republican Town Committee, Hanover, $300; Ripon Society, $500.

Trent Lott (Miss.), $23,392: Associated General Contractors Construction Committee for Action, $500; Committee for Thorough Agricultural Political Education, $500; American Conservative Union Victory Fund, $5,500; Friends of Trent Lott Committee, $2,317; Mississippi Political Action Committee, $2,500; National Republican Congressional Committee, $500; Republican Committee, Pearl River County, $425; Republican National Boosters Club, $10,000; Republican Party, Jones County, $150; SPACE, $1,000.

Harold V. Froehlich (Wis.), $50,395: American Conservative Union Victory Fund, $5,700; Associated General Contractors Committee for Action, $750; BIPAC, $3,000; National Board of Life Underwriters Political Action Committee, $450; National Association of Real Estate Boards Political Action Committee, $1,100; Republican Congressional Boosters Club, $10,000; Republican Party, Marinette County, $200; Republican Party, Waupaca County, $995; Republican Party of Wisconsin, $20,200; Republican Voluntary Committee, Brown County, $2,500; WISPAC (Wisconsin branch, AMA), $5,500.

Carlos J. Moorhead (Calif.), $30,003: BIPAC, $1,000; California Medical Political Action Committee (California branch, AMA), $10,000; California Real Estate Association, 43rd District, $300; California Savings and Loan Association Century Club, $500; Fluor Construction Corporation Employees Political Fund, $500; General Telephone and Electronics Good Government Club, $300; Good Government Association, $300; National Association of Real Estate Boards Political Education Committee, $500; Republican Club, Sierra Madre, $550; Republican Congressional Boosters Club, $10,000; Republican Women's Club, Altadena, $350; Republican Women's Club, Arcadia, $250; Republican Women's Club, East Pasadena, Sierra Madre, $300; Republican Women's Study Club, Glendale, $452; Republican Women's Workshop, Glendale, $200; Republican Women's Club, La Canada Valley, $250; Republican Women's Club, Los Feliz, $800; Republican Women's Club, San Marino, $195; Union Bank Good Government Association, $200; Union Oil Political Awareness Fund, $250; Union Pacific Fund for Effective Government, $200; United Congressional Appeal, $1,500; United Republicans of California, Foothill Unit #23, $250; Wells Fargo Company Good Government Committee, $500; Young Republican Club, $356.

Joseph J. Maraziti (N.J.), $15,500: BIPAC, $2,000; JEMPAC (New Jersey branch, AMA), $2,500; Johnson and Johnson Good Government Fund, $500; National Association of Real Estate Boards Political Education Committee, $500; Republican Congressional Boosters Club, $10,000.

Delbert L. Latta (Ohio), $15,500: American Importers Association, American International Trade Political Affairs Committee (AITPAC), $200; National Republican Congressional Committee, $4,300; Ohio Contractors Political Action Committee, $500; Ohio Medical Political Action Committee (Ohio branch, AMA), $1,500; Republican State Central and Executive Committee, $9,000.

(Precedents story continued from p. 14)

What happens if an official about to be impeached resigns his office?

In general, this puts an end to impeachment proceedings since the primary objective, removal from office, has been accomplished. This was the case in the impeachment proceedings begun against two federal judges—Mark H. Delahay, impeached by voice vote Feb. 28, 1873, and George W. English, impeached by a 306-62 vote April 1, 1926.

However, resignation is not a foolproof way of precluding impeachment. Secretary of War William W. Belknap, aware of the findings of a congressional committee implicating him in the acceptance of bribes, resigned at 10 o'clock on the morning of March 2, 1876. Sometime after 3 o'clock that afternoon, the House impeached him by voice vote. The Senate debated the question of its jurisdiction, in light of his resignation, and decided by a vote of 37-29 that he could be impeached and tried despite his no longer being in office. He was found not guilty of the charges.

What happens to impeachment proceedings in progress when Congress adjourns?

Historical precedent indicates that an impeachment proceeding does not die with adjournment. In 1890-91 the Judiciary Committee investigated the conduct of a federal judge and decided that he should be impeached; a resolution to that effect was reported in 1891 and the House began debate, but did not conclude it before adjournment. In the new Congress in 1892, the evidence taken in the first investigation was referred to the committee again, a second investigation was conducted and the committee decided against impeachment.

In the case of the impeachment of Judge Pickering, the House impeached him, but adjourned before drawing up articles of impeachment, which a committee appointed in the next Congress did do.

Whether impeachment would have to begin again if the House impeached a man in one Congress, but the Senate trial could not begin until the next is unclear —although the view of the Senate as a continuing body according to custom, would indicate that the trial could begin in new Congress without a repetition of the House procedures. The Senate did decide in 1876 that a trial of impeachment could proceed only when Congress was in session. The vote was 21-19.

DOAR AND JENNER HEAD LARGE, YOUNG AND BUSY STAFF

It is the youngest, largest and busiest of Washington's special legal teams. Its mission is to ascertain whether proper grounds exist for the House of Representatives to impeach, and the Senate to remove from office, President Richard M. Nixon.

The outcome and historic impact of the inquiry depends heavily on the integrity of the investigation conducted by the 43 attorneys of the House Judiciary Committee's special staff.

If the evidence they produce is judged sufficient to justify impeachment by the committee members, the House and the nation, then their findings will form the case for the prosecution, the case which House members will have to take to the Senate for trial. Should the staff have failed in that task, and the House members find themselves standing before the Senate inadequately equipped, they would be "up the creek without a paddle," as one Judiciary Committee Republican has warned.

So who are these lawyers hard at work on the second floor of the converted hotel behind the House office buildings? Where do they come from and what are their qualifications for this almost unprecedented task?

The answers are not easy to find. Extensive security arrangements insulate the attorneys from the public, the press and even from members of Congress. Their names and basic biographical data were made public by special counsel John M. Doar Feb. 5. But further inquiries concerning which were selected by Republicans, which headed the six task forces investigating various types of charges against the President, and which attorneys were working in which subject areas, were all met with the response that that information was to remain confidential—to protect staff members from possible harassment or pressure.

Even as Doar was selecting his staff, he barred all contact with the press, fearful of the news leaks which had resulted in so many front page stories during the investigations by the Senate Watergate Committee. He appointed Donald Coppock, a veteran of 32 years with the Border Patrol of the Justice Department's Immigration and Naturalization Service, to handle press relations for the inquiry staff.

And rules adopted Feb. 22 for the staff stated plainly: "The staff of the impeachment inquiry shall not discuss with anyone outside the staff either the substance or procedure of their work or that of the committee." *(Box p. 34)*

A Youthful Profile

Despite the tight lid on information, the basic data provided allows a profile of the staff to be traced. It resembles a newly organized, medium-size Washington law firm headed by two distinguished senior partners of wide reputation, with a few younger partners and a large number of associates only recently graduated from law school. The age range is from 66 to 25; the average age is 33. The salary range is from $36,000 to $14,000.

Compared to the other special legal teams in town, the impeachment inquiry staff is large. When supporting personnel—investigators, secretaries, clerks—are added to the 43 lawyers, the total is close to 100. With that weight, it outnumbers the 38 members of the House Judiciary Committee, all of whom are lawyers, the 17 attorneys and 64 total staff of the Senate Watergate Committee, and the 38 lawyers and 80 total staff of the special Watergate prosecutor's office.

The 43 attorneys selected—actually 41 when Doar and minority counsel Albert E. Jenner Jr. are excepted—were chosen from more than 400 applications. A dozen were selected by Jenner and the minority members of the committee, the remainder by Doar and the Democrats on the committee. The average age of those selected by the Republicans—36—is slightly above that of the Democratic choices—32.

The Leaders. Jenner, a Chicago attorney of considerable renown in legal circles, is the most senior and experienced member of the staff. Senior partner of the firm with which he has practiced for more than 40 years, Jenner looks younger than his 66 years, with his stylishly long silver sideburns, his well-tailored dark-striped suits and print bow ties.

Jenner had declined when asked by Judiciary Committee Chairman Peter W. Rodino Jr. (D N.J.) late in 1973 to consider the post of special counsel. Doar later accepted the position. Later, Jenner said, he accepted the post of minority counsel only after "the Illinois boys worked hard on me," presumably referring to Robert McClory (R Ill.) and Tom Railsback (R Ill.), the two Illinois Republicans on the Judiciary Committee.

The unity and bipartisan nature of the staff has been emphasized from the beginning of the inquiry, and blurring of party lines within the staff has been facilitated by the fact that neither Doar nor Jenner fits neatly into a party label. Jenner, a Republican, is also a lifelong

(Continued on p. 33)

John M. Doar

Albert E. Jenner Jr.

Two Distinguished Senior Partners

Impeachable Offense: Opinion of Inquiry Staff

Following are excerpts from a Feb. 20 memorandum prepared by the impeachment inquiry staff of the House Judiciary Committee (See p. 38 for contrasting views of President Nixon's attorneys):

The Historical Origins of the Impeachment Process

"The Constitution provides that the President '...shall be removed from Office on Impeachment for, and Conviction of, Treason, Bribery, or other high Crimes and Misdemeanors.' The framers could have written simply 'or other crimes'.... They did not do that .... They adopted instead a unique phrase used for centuries in English parliamentary impeachments....

"Two points emerge from the 400 years of English parliamentary experience with the phrase.... First, the particular allegations of misconduct, alleged damage to the state in such forms as misapplication of funds, abuse of official power, neglect of duty, encroachment on Parliament's prerogatives, corruption, and betrayal of trust. Second, the phrase...was confined to parliamentary impeachments; it had no roots in the ordinary criminal law, and the particular allegations of misconduct under that heading were not necessarily limited to common law or statutory derelictions or crimes.

"**The Intention of the Framers.** The debates on impeachment at the Constitutional Convention...focus principally on its applicability to the President.... Impeachment was to be one of the central elements of executive responsibility....

"The framers intended impeachment to be a constitutional safeguard of the public trust, the powers of government conferred upon the President...and the division of powers....

"**The American Impeachment Cases.** ...Does Article III, Section 1 of the Constitution, which states that judges 'shall hold their Offices during good Behavior,' limit the relevance of the ten impeachments of judges with respect to presidential impeachment standards as has been argued...? It does not....

"Each of the thirteen American impeachments involved charges of misconduct incompatible with the official position of the officeholder. This conduct falls into three broad categories: (1) exceeding the constitutional bounds of the powers of the office in derogation of the powers of another branch of government; (2) behaving in a manner grossly incompatible with the proper function and purpose of the office; and (3) employing the power of the office for an improper purpose or for personal gain....

"In drawing up articles of impeachment, the House has placed little emphasis on criminal conduct. Less than one-third of the eighty-three articles the House has adopted have explicitly charged the violation of a criminal statute or used the word 'criminal' or 'crime' to describe the conduct alleged....

"Much more common in the articles are allegations that the officer has violated his duties or his oath or seriously undermined public confidence in his ability to perform his official functions....

"All have involved charges of conduct incompatible with continued performance of the office; some have explicitly rested upon a 'course of conduct'.... Some of the individual articles seem to have alleged conduct that, taken alone, would not have been considered serious....

The Criminality Issue

"The central issue...is whether requiring an indictable offense as an essential element of impeachable conduct is consistent with the purposes and intent of the framers....

"Impeachment and the criminal law serve fundamentally different purposes. Impeachment is the first step in a remedial process.... The purpose...is not personal punishment; its function is primarily to maintain constitutional government....

"The general applicability of the criminal law also makes it inappropriate as the standard.... In an impeachment proceeding a President is called to account for abusing powers which only a President possesses.

"Impeachable conduct...may include the serious failure to discharge the affirmative duties imposed on the President by the Constitution. Unlike a criminal case, the cause for removal...may be based on his entire course of conduct in office.... It may be a course of conduct more than individual acts that has a tendency to subvert constitutional government.

"To confine impeachable conduct to indictable offenses may well be to set a standard so restrictive as not to reach conduct that might adversely affect the system of government. Some of the most grievous offenses against our constitutional form of government may not entail violations of the criminal law....

"To limit impeachable conduct to criminal offenses would be incompatible with the evidence...and would frustrate the purpose that the framers intended....

Conclusion

"In the English practice and in several of the American impeachments, the criminality issue was not raised at all. The emphasis has been on the significant effects of the conduct....Impeachment was evolved... to cope with both the inadequacy of criminal standards and the impotence of the courts to deal with the conduct of great public figures. It would be anomalous if the framers, having barred criminal sanctions from the impeachment remedy...intended to restrict the grounds for impeachment to conduct that was criminal.

"The longing for precise criteria is understandable.... However, where the issue is presidential compliance with the constitutional requirements and limitations on the presidency, the crucial factor is not the intrinsic quality of behavior but the significance of its effects upon our constitutional system or the functioning of our government."

(Continued from p. 31)

Committee Staff: The Chiefs

John M. Doar, 52, special counsel in charge of impeachment inquiry staff: Minnesota native; graduate of University of California at Berkeley Law School, 1949; veteran of seven years in the Justice Department's civil rights division, the last two as assistant attorney general heading the division; selected as special counsel by Committee Chairman Peter W. Rodino Jr.; selection announced Dec. 20, 1973.

Albert E. Jenner Jr., 66, minority counsel selected early in January 1974: Chicago native; graduate of the University of Illinois Law School, 1930; senior partner of Chicago firm of Jenner and Block; veteran of 42 years practice of law.

Joseph A. Woods Jr., 48, senior associate special counsel in charge of constitutional and legal research: Alabama-born; classmate of Doar's at law school; California resident on leave from Oakland law firm of Donahue, Gallagher, Thomas and Woods, with which he has practiced since 1950.

Samuel Garrison III, 32, deputy minority counsel: native of Roanoke, Virginia; graduate of the University of Virginia Law School, 1966; former commonwealth's attorney for the city of Roanoke; associate minority counsel for the House Judiciary Committee, and special assistant to former Vice President Agnew; selected by the Republicans to work on the impeachment inquiry; began work Dec. 1, 1973.

Richard L. Cates, 48, senior associate special counsel overseeing factual research: graduate of the University of Wisconsin Law School, 1951; senior partner of Madison law firm of Lawton & Cates; on leave to work with the committee since Nov. 11, 1973.

Bernard W. Nussbaum, 36, senior associate special counsel overseeing factual research: New York native; graduate of Harvard Law School, 1961; former assistant U.S. attorney for the southern district of New York; partner in New York law firm of Wachtell, Lipton, Rosen & Katz.

Robert D. Sack, 34, senior counsel: Philadelphia native; graduate of Columbia University Law School, 1963; partner in Wall Street firm of Patterson, Belknap & Webb.

Robert A. Shelton, 32, senior counsel in charge of office security and management: Atlanta native; graduate of Harvard Law School, 1966; recently named partner of Baltimore firm of Venable, Baetjer, and Howard.

Richard H. Gill, 33, senior counsel: Alabama native; graduate of University of Virginia Law School, 1965; on leave of absence from the Montgomery law firm of Hobbs, Copeland, Franco & Screws.

Evan A. Davis, 30, senior counsel: New York native; graduate of Columbia Law School, 1969; former law clerk to Justice Potter Stewart; general counsel for New York City budget bureau and chief of the consumer protection division of the New York City Law Department.

friend of the family of the present Democratic senator from Illinois, Adlai E. Stevenson III, for whom he has attended at least one fund-raising dinner.

Doar, 52, practiced law with his family firm in New Richmond, Wis., during the 1950s, coming to Washington in the last days of the Eisenhower administration to join the newly created civil rights division of the Justice Department. Although a Republican by background, Doar stayed on into the crisis-filled civil rights days during the Kennedy and Johnson administrations, rising to head the division from 1965 until he left it in 1967. After six years of service in New York City, first as a member and president of the city school board and later as head of the Bedford-Stuyvesant Corporation, Doar was recalled to Washington to head the impeachment inquiry.

A tall, thin man with short graying curly hair and wire rim glasses, Doar speaks carefully and quietly with the air of a weary college professor. His clothes match his demeanor—conservative dark suits, white shirts and dark ties. But Doar is renowned for working days and nights with little rest.

The Deputies. Only one other member of the staff besides Doar is in his fifties, and only four are in their forties. Two of those are Joseph A. Woods, Jr., a classmate of Doar's at University of California Law School who left his Oakland law practice to head the constitutional and legal research unit of the impeachment inquiry staff, and Richard L. Cates, an attorney who took leave from his Madison, Wis., law firm to join the impeachment staff early in November 1973. Cates, with Bernard W. Nussbaum, 36, a New York lawyer, oversees the six task forces engaged in factual research.

Serving as Jenner's administrative deputy is Samuel Garrison III, 32, who joined the staff early in December, handling much of the minority's selection of staff attorneys. A native of the Virginia congressional district which sent Richard H. Poff (R Va. 1953-72) and then M. Caldwell Butler (R Va.) to Congress and the Judiciary Committee, Garrison joined the staff after working as congressional liaison on the Senate staff of Vice President Spiro T. Agnew.

The Staff. Of the other members of the staff, one—Edward S. Szukelewicz, a veteran of 22 years service in the Justice Department, chiefly in criminal investigation and prosecution—is in his fifties. Two attorneys other than Woods and Cates—Dagmar S. Hamilton, who served in the civil rights division with Doar, and John Edward Kennahan, former commonwealth's attorney for the city of Alexandria, Va.—are in their forties.

Of the remaining 34 members, half are in their thirties and half in their twenties. Eight of the latter are members of the law school class of 1973.

Described as senior counsel are four of the other attorneys: Robert D. Sack, who came to the staff from a Wall Street law firm; Robert A. Shelton, who came from a Baltimore firm; Richard H. Gill, a Montgomery, Ala., attorney who attended the University of Virginia Law School with Garrison, and Evan A. Davis, former chief of the consumer protection division of the New York City Law Department.

Shelton, a recently appointed partner in the law firm with which committee member Paul S. Sarbanes (D Md.) formerly was associated, is in charge of the physical functioning of the office, but the duties of the other three senior counsel are unspecified.

(Continued on p. 35)

House Judiciary Committee Staff: The Indians

Fred H. Altshuler, 30, Detroit native; 1968 graduate of University of Chicago Law School; four years' work with California Rural Legal Assistance.

Thomas D. Bell, 28, Missouri native; 1971 graduate of the University of Wisconsin Law School; on leave from position held since 1972 as associate with the Doar family firm—Doar, Drill, Norman & Bakke.

William Paul Bishop, 26, Atlanta native; 1973 graduate of the University of Georgia Law School.

Robert L. Brown, 26, Alabama native; 1973 graduate of Rutgers Law School.

Michael M. Conway, 27, Missouri native; 1973 graduate of Yale Law School; on leave of absence from Chicago firm of Hopkins, Sutter, Owen, Mulroy & Davis.

Rufus Cormier Jr., 25, Texan and 1973 graduate of Yale Law School; on leave of absence from New York law firm of Paul, Weiss, Rifkind, Wharton & Garrison.

E. Lee Dale, 30, native of Pittsburgh; 1968 graduate of Vanderbilt Law School; practiced law with Denver firm of Dawson, Nagel, Sherman & Howard.

John B. Davidson, 30, native of Chicago; graduate of Harvard Business School and Harvard Law School, 1972; on leave of absence from employment with Chicago firm of Louis G. Davidson and Associates.

Chris Gekas, 27, Chicago native; 1970 graduate of the University of Illinois Law School; former member of legislation and special projects section of the criminal division, Department of Justice.

Dagmar S. Hamilton, 42, Philadelphia native; 1961 graduate of American University Law School; lawyer in civil rights division of Justice Department (1965-66); lecturer in Department of Government, University of Texas (1966-73).

David Gordon Hanes, 32, New York native; 1969 graduate of Columbia Law School; former senior law clerk to Chief Justice Warren E. Burger; associate with Washington firm of Wilmer, Cutler & Pickering.

John Edward Kennahan, 49, New York native; graduate of Georgetown University Law Center; former commonwealth's attorney for Alexandria, Va. (1969-73).

Terry Rhodes Kirkpatrick, 26, Virginia native; 1972 graduate of University of Arkansas Law School; special assistant for criminal matters, Arkansas Supreme Court.

John R. Labovitz, 30, native of Washington, D.C.; 1969 graduate of University of Chicago Law School; staff of President's Commission on Campus Unrest; research associate, Brookings Institution.

Lawrence Lucchino, 28, Pittsburgh native; 1972 graduate of Yale Law School.

R. L. Smith McKeithen, 30, North Carolina native; 1971 graduate of Columbia Law School; associate with Wall Street firm of Shearman and Sterling.

Robert Paul Murphy, 27, Maine native; 1973 graduate of Columbia Law School; formerly attorney-adviser with General Accounting Office.

James B. F. Oliphant, 35, New York native; 1966 graduate of University of Colorado Law School; veteran of four years' service in the organized crime and racketeering section of the criminal division, Justice Department (1968-72).

Richard H. Porter, 25, 1972 graduate of Yale Law School; associate with Milwaukee law firm of Foley and Lardner.

George G. Rayborn Jr., 36, Mississippi native; 1963 graduate of Rutgers Law School; three years' service with the Justice Department (1964-67); federal public defender in Los Angeles (1972-74).

James M. Reum, 27, Illinois native; 1972 graduate of Harvard Law School; associate with New York firm of Davis, Polk & Wardwell.

Hillary Rodham, 26, Chicago native; graduate of Yale Law School; formerly with Children's Defense Fund of the Washington Research Project.

Stephen A. Sharp, 26, Ohioan; 1973 graduate of University of Virginia Law School; law clerk and then attorney in office of general counsel, Federal Communications Commission.

Jared Stamell, 27, Detroit native; 1971 graduate of Harvard Law School; member of judiciary committee staff since early 1973 after year of service in Justice Department.

Roscoe B. Starek, III, 26, Minnesota native; 1973 graduate of American University Law School; member of staff of Sen. Charles H. Percy (R Ill.), then of staff of Senate Permanent Subcommittee on Investigations, and then of Federal Energy Office.

Garry William Sutton, 30, born in Canada; 1969 graduate of Harvard Law School; associate with Wall Street firm of Shearman and Sterling.

Edward S. Szukelewicz, 57, Brooklyn-born; 1940 graduate of St. John's University School of Law; veteran of 22 years' service in the Justice Department, criminal division.

Theodore Robert Tetzlaff, 30, Milwaukee native; 1969 graduate of Yale Law School; former associate acting director of legal services, Office of Economic Opportunity (1972-73); on leave from post as associate with Chicago firm of Jenner and Block.

Robert James Trainor, 27, New York native; 1971 graduate of Villanova Law School; member of committee staff since July 30, 1973, after serving as staff member for House Select Crime Committee.

Jean LaRue Traylor Jr., 36, Buffalo native; graduate of State University of New York at Buffalo Law School; formerly with criminal section of civil rights division of Justice Department.

Ben A. Wallis Jr., 37, Texan; 1966 graduate of University of Texas Law School; formerly vice president for development, Club Corporation of America.

William Floyd Weld, 28, New York native; 1970 graduate of Harvard Law School; associate with Boston firm of Hill and Barlow.

William Anthony White, 33, native of Washington, D.C.; 1969 graduate of Northwestern Law School; former U.S. attorney, District of Columbia (1970-73).

(Continued from p. 33)

Education, Experience

Harvard, Yale and Columbia Law Schools can claim the largest number of alumni on the impeachment inquiry staff, with seven, six and five attorneys, respectively. Seventeen other law schools are represented, from California (Doar and Woods) to the University of Illinois, Jenner's law school, to Rutgers and Villanova.

Four of the staff attorneys are black: Robert L. Brown, a 1973 graduate of Rutgers Law School, which is located in Newark—hometown of House Judiciary Committee Chairman Peter W. Rodino Jr. (D N.J.); Rufus Cormier Jr., a native of Beaumont, Texas, hometown of senior committee Democrat Jack Brooks (D Texas), and a 1973 graduate of Yale Law School; Richard H. Porter, a 1972 graduate of Yale Law School; and Jean LaRue Traylor Jr., who came to the staff from the Justice Department's civil rights division.

And two of the staff attorneys are women: Hamilton, who served in the civil rights division with Doar before moving to Austin, Texas, where she taught at the University of Texas, and Hillary Rodham, a recent graduate of Yale Law School.

Experience. Despite their description by Rodino and Edward Hutchinson (R Mich.), the committee's rank-ing Republican member, as "professional" and "highly qualified," only slightly more than half of the legal staff have actually engaged in the private practice of law during the last 10 years. Of these, 15 have practiced law for only three years or less. They come from several New York and Chicago law firms, and also from Milwaukee, Boston, Denver, Montgomery, Oakland and Baltimore. From the Doar family firm in New Richmond, Wis., came a young associate, Thomas D. Bell; from Jenner's Chicago law firm came another, Theodore Robert Tetzlaff.

Doar, Garrison and 14 of the other lawyers came to the staff from some sort of government or public service; three others came from legal aid work; one from teaching and one from business. Eight have had Justice Department experience: Doar, Hamilton, Szukelewicz, Traylor, Chris Gekas, James B. F. Oliphant, George G. Rayborn Jr., and Jared Stamell.

Republican Selections. Approximately one-third of the attorneys selected for the staff were chosen by Jenner, Garrison and the minority members of the committee. Besides Jenner and Garrison, they were Gekas, Szukelewicz, Tetzlaff, John Edward Kennahan, Oliphant, James M. Reum, Stephen A. Sharp, Roscoe B. Starek III, Ben A. Wallis Jr., William Floyd Weld and William Anthony White.

Relevant experience was clearly a criteria in the selection of these attorneys. From a background of prosecutorial experience come Garrison, who served as commonwealth's attorney for Roanoke, Va.; Kennahan, defeated in 1973 in his bid for a second term as commonwealth's attorney for Alexandria, Va.; White, who came from the office of the U.S. attorney for the District of Columbia, the office which initially prosecuted the Watergate burglars; Oliphant, Szukelewicz, and Wallis.

Adding political know-how are Garrison, fresh from the office of the vice president, and Starek, who joined the staff after working with Sen. Charles H. Percy (R Ill.), the Senate Permanent Subcommittee on Investigations, and the Federal Energy Office.

Tetzlaff is not an unknown in Washington, having served briefly as chief of legal services for the Office of Economic Opportunity, until he was fired early in 1973 by Howard J. Phillips, appointed acting OEO director by President Nixon to dismantle that office.

Cost. The largest chunk of the $1-million which the House provided to the committee in November to fund the initial months of the impeachment inquiry was for salaries.

The top six men on the inquiry staff—Doar, Jenner, Garrison, Woods, Cates and Nussbaum—are each paid at an annual rate of $36,000. No other salary levels were revealed.

But semi-annual reports, printed in the *Congressional Record* early in 1974, gave some indication of the salary level of those who already had joined the staff in 1973. Top among them was Kennahan, an experienced attorney, who was paid at an annual rate of about $26,-000 for the month that he worked for the inquiry staff in 1973. Robert James Trainor and Jared Stamell, both hired earlier in the year, were paid about $21,000 a year, while Traylor and Brown, who came to work the Monday after the "Saturday Night Massacre"—Oct. 23, 1973—were paid at an annual rate of about $18,000.

Staff Rules

Following are the staff rules adopted by the House Judiciary Committee Feb. 22:

The chairman and the ranking minority member have made the following rules for the staff:

1. The staff of the impeachment inquiry shall not discuss with anyone outside the staff either the substance or procedure of their work or that of the committee.

2. Staff offices on the second floor of the congressional annex shall operate under strict security precautions. One guard shall be on duty at all times by the elevator to control entry. All persons entering the floor shall identify themselves. An additional guard shall be posted at night for surveillance of the secure area where sensitive documents are kept.

3. Sensitive documents and other things shall be segregated in a secure storage area. They may be examined only at supervised reading facilities within the secure area. Copying or duplicating of such documents and other things is prohibited.

4. Access to classified information supplied to the committee shall be limited by the special counsel and the counsel to the minority to those staff members with appropriate security clearances and a need to know.

5. Testimony taken or papers and things received by the staff shall not be disclosed or made public by the staff unless authorized by a majority of the committee.

6. Executive session transcripts and records shall be available to designated committee staff for inspection in person but may not be released or disclosed to any other person without the consent of a majority of the committee.

A SMALL NIXON DEFENSE TEAM HAS RECRUITING PROBLEMS

By the end of March 1973, less than six weeks before the special House Judiciary Committee staff was due to report on whether proper grounds existed for the impeachment of President Nixon, the White House legal defense team had one particularly salient feature.

It was small.

James D. St. Clair, the experienced Boston trial lawyer who would most likely defend Nixon in a Senate impeachment trial, had only four staff lawyers working for him as of March 21, compared to the 43 lawyers on the Judiciary Committee's impeachment study staff.

Counting staffs of the Senate Watergate Committee and special prosecutor Leon Jaworski, the White House faced an array of almost 150 adversaries.

St. Clair had the services of one other full-time lawyer, special counsel to the President John J. Chester, and a $100-a-day consultant, Jerome J. Murphy. Counting St. Clair and the four staff lawyers, this brought the active impeachment defense team to a grand total of seven.

Also listed by the White House as members of the legal team were J. Fred Buzhardt Jr., counsel to the President; presidential Assistant Leonard Garment, and consultants Charles A. Wright, Thomas P. Marinis and Samuel J. Powers. (Box, this page)

However, White House spokesmen acknowledged that none of these was actively involved in the impeachment duel with the Judiciary Committee staff.

Casualty Rate

The casualty rate among White House lawyers had been high.

With the March 15 departure of Robert T. Andrews, a 54-year-old lawyer who had been the senior member of St. Clair's staff, the dismantling of the original Watergate legal defense team that had come in with Buzhardt on May 10, 1973, was complete. "I only stayed over to help with the transition," said Andrews, who returned to his former job as deputy assistant general counsel for the Defense Department.

The first victim was presidential counsel John W. Dean III, whom Nixon fired April 30, 1973, charging that he had withheld information from the President about the Watergate coverup.

The next was Wright, who had come to the White House to construct a constitutional argument supporting Nixon's refusal to turn over Watergate tapes and documents to Judge John J. Sirica and the Watergate grand jury. Wright returned to his post as a law professor at the University of Texas shortly after Nixon reversed his stand on the tapes in the wake of the Oct. 20 firing of special Watergate prosecutor Archibald Cox. Amid what the White House called a "firestorm" of public reaction to the

Consultants

Jerome J. Murphy, 31, consultant to the President since Dec. 15, 1973, $100 a day; a native of St. Louis, Mo. Murphy was a 1964 graduate of Notre Dame University and received a law degree from St. Louis University in 1968. He was an assistant U.S. attorney and district counsel for the Drug Enforcement Administration Task Force in St. Louis before joining the White House team.

Also listed as consultants but not active in the impeachment fight as of early March 1974 were:

Charles A. Wright, 46, consultant to the President since June 6, 1973, $150 a day; law professor at the University of Texas.

Thomas P. Marinis Jr., 30, consultant to the President since June 6, 1973, $150 a day; member of the Houston law firm of Vinson, Elkins, Searls, Connally & Smith and a former student of Wright.

Samuel J. Powers, 56, consultant to the President since Nov. 5, 1973, $150 a day; a member of the Miami, Fla., law firm of Blackwell, Walker & Green.

firing, and demands in Congress for impeachment, Nixon announced that he would release the tapes.

The next ones to go were Buzhardt and Garment, who headed the legal team until St. Clair took over on Jan. 5. They were both promoted out of the job after Buzhardt became a target of criticism within the administration following his handling of the mysterious gaps that appeared in the tapes that Nixon finally turned over to Sirica. Buzhardt testified before Sirica on Nov. 29 that when he first discovered the 18½-minute gap in a conversation between Nixon and aide H. R. Haldeman, recorded three days after the Watergate break-in, Buzhardt did not think there was any "innocent explanation" for it.

Recruiting Problems. As Andrews left, St. Clair was preparing to hire "five or six" more staff lawyers, some or all of them from the civil division of the Justice Department, Congressional Quarterly learned.

St. Clair could not be reached to answer why the staff additions were coming so late. However, a spokesman for St. Clair told Congressional Quarterly, "I don't think anyone really has had much time to actively go out and recruit staff lawyers. It's sort of catch as catch can around here because everybody's so darned busy."

The White House had not been very successful in attracting new staffers. Congressional Quarterly learned that St. Clair's predecessor, Buzhardt, had invited applications from at least two repositories of government lawyers—the U.S. attorney's office for the District of Colum-

Tax Lawyers

H. Chapman Rose, 67, donating his services as a tax consultant to President Nixon, according to a White House spokesman. Rose served in the Eisenhower administration as assistant secretary of the treasury (1953-55) and as under secretary of the treasury (1955-56). He was a partner in the 137-member Cleveland, Ohio, law firm of Jones, Day, Cockley & Reavis, which specialized in corporation, tax, trust and estate planning law. Clients included Chrysler, General Motors and Republic Steel. A native of Columbus, Ohio, Rose was a 1928 graduate of Princeton University. He received a law degree from Harvard University in 1931 and served as secretary to Supreme Court Justice Oliver Wendell Holmes in 1931 and 1932.

Kenneth W. Gemmill, 64, also donating his services as a tax consultant, according to the White House. Gemmil was an assistant to the treasury secretary under the Eisenhower administration in 1953 and 1954 and was acting chief counsel of the Internal Revenue Service in 1953. He was a partner in the 118-member law firm of Dechert, Price & Rhoads with main offices in Philadelphia and branches in Harrisburg, Pa., Washington, D.C., and Brussels, Belgium. Born in Ivyland, Pa., Gemmil was a 1932 graduate of Princeton University and received a law degree from the University of Pennsylvania in 1935.

Preparers. The consultants who prepared Nixon's tax returns were Frank DeMarco, a member of the firm of Kalmbach, DeMarco, Knapp & Chillingworth of Los Angeles and Newport Beach, Calif., and Arthur Blech, a certified public accountant with his own firm in Los Angeles.

bia and the Justice Department's office of legal counsel. The office of legal counsel had been responsible for preparing a lengthy study of impeachment under the direction of then Acting Attorney General Robert H. Bork, which was partly the reason for the White House interest.

No one from the office of legal counsel volunteered, and only one person signed on from the U.S. attorney's office: John A. McCahill, a 34-year-old assistant U.S. attorney who had been planning to leave government service and go into private law practice. McCahill joined the staff Nov. 27, 1973.

"It looked like just the most exciting case of the century regardless of what your political viewpoints are," McCahill told Congressional Quarterly. "They explained to me that it would be a strictly professional job and I would not be part of the political staff. I would be a lawyer doing work as if I were in a private law firm. I took it on that basis and that's the way it's been. I think it's a privilege to be involved in a case of this magnitude."

Of those contacted, the lawyers who decided to pass up the job cited two main reasons: fear of not being able to return to their jobs once their stint with St. Clair had ended, and a general conviction among many that Nixon was not telling his attorneys the full extent of his involvement in Watergate.

At a meeting with reporters March 20, Attorney General William B. Saxbe deplored this attitude and assured Justice Department lawyers that they could volunteer for assignment to the White House on the understanding that their jobs would be waiting for them when they returned.

"I'm astounded sometimes by the attitude that people have that the President is not entitled to defend himself," Saxbe said.

Evidently many of the lawyers were unconvinced.

'Have to Be Nuts.' "I think you'd have to be nuts to work there (in the White House)," one lawyer said. "I think some of Nixon's past lawyers, like Wright and Buzhardt, have really been hurt. A smart client in a murder case will come to you and tell you what he did, how he did it, why he did it, and you can deal with the evidence. But when every day you think of a strategy and the prosecution comes out with some document that your client never told you they had, and knocks you off at the pass, you don't look too good as a lawyer. At least you expect them to level with you, and the White House is liable to leave you dangling in the wind, as they put it."

A lawyer who said he was tempted by the offer declared, "I wanted at least to consider it overnight. I don't know how many times I would have the opportunity to work in the White House. But I think the proper role for a lawyer is to believe in his client..."

"Most of the people in this office are young and only two or three years out of law school," said another lawyer. "If they got into a situation that was over their heads, it could really damage their careers. I'm speaking for myself, too."

Though St. Clair could not be reached for comment, former senior staff member Andrews acknowledged that the White House had encountered trouble assembling a suitable staff.

"We had some overzealous applicants, and they aren't so good," Andrews said. "And there was a feeling on the part of some that somehow they would be tied to their client. I think it's unfortunate that some people feel this way. Even a bad guy or somebody who's been up the river before is entitled to representation, and the man who represents him is not considered a bad guy too."

Other Staffers. In addition to McCahill, St. Clair's staff as of March 19 consisted of:

• Cecil Emerson, 39, a former assistant district attorney and assistant U.S. attorney in Dallas, Texas, and regional director of the Dallas Drug Enforcement Administration Task Force before joining the White House team Nov. 25, 1973;

• Michael Sterlacci, 31, who was assistant general counsel of the United States Information Agency (USIA) before coming to the White House Dec. 10, 1973; and

• Loren A. Smith, 29, who worked in the general counsel's office of the Federal Communications Commission (FCC) before signing with St. Clair Nov. 27, 1973.

Salaries. The mechanism by which McCahill's and Sterlacci's salaries were being paid was somewhat unusual.

With the exception of Emerson, who was being paid from White House funds, the staff lawyers were classified as agency employees "detailed" to the White House—a practice whereby the White House obtained staffers without having to pay them out of the White House budget.

(Continued on p. 39)

Impeachable Offense: Opinion of Nixon Attorneys

Following are excerpts from a Feb. 28 analysis prepared by James D. St. Clair, John J. Chester, Michael A. Sterlacci, Jerome J. Murphy and Loren A. Smith, attorneys for President Nixon:

English Background of Constitutional Impeachment Provisions

"The Framers felt that the English system permitted men...to make arbitrary decisions, and one of their primary purposes in creating a Constitution was to replace this arbitrariness with a system based on the rule of law.... They felt impeachment was a necessary check on a President who might commit a crime, but they did not want to see the vague standards of the English system that made impeachment a weapon to achieve parliamentary supremacy....

"To argue that the President may be impeached for something less than a criminal offense, with all the safeguards that definition implies, would be a monumental step backwards into all those old English practices that our Constitution sought to eliminate. American impeachment was not designed to force a President into surrendering executive authority...but to check overtly criminal actions as they are defined by law....

"The terminology 'high crimes and misdemeanors' should create no confusion or ambiguity.... It was a unitary phrase meaning crimes against the state, as opposed to those against individuals.... It is as ridiculous to say that 'misdemeanor' must mean something beyond 'crime' as it is to suggest that in the phrase 'bread and butter issues' butter issues must be different from bread issues....

The Constitutional Convention

"It is evident from the actual debate and from the events leading up to it that Morris' remark that 'An election of every four years will prevent maladministration,' expressed the will of the Convention. Thus, the impeachment provision adopted was designed to deal exclusively with indictable criminal conduct.... The Convention rejected all non-criminal definitions of impeachable offenses.... To distort the clear meaning of the phrase 'treason, bribery or other high crimes and misdemeanors' by including non-indictable conduct would thus most certainly violate the Framers' intent."

Legal Meaning of Impeachment Provision

"Just as statutes are to be construed to uphold the intent of the drafters...so should we uphold the intent of the drafters of the Constitution that impeachable offenses be limited to criminal violations. Also as penal statutes have been strictly construed in favor of the accused, so should we construe the impeachment provisions of the Constitution....

American Impeachment Precedents

"Some of the proponents of presidential impeachment place great emphasis on the cases involving federal judges to support the proposition that impeachment will lie for conduct which does not of itself constitute an indictable offense. This view is apparently most appealing to those broad constructionists who favoring a severely weakened Chief Executive argue that certain non-criminal 'political' offenses may justify impeachment....

"The Framers...distinguished between the President and judges concerning the standard to be employed for an impeachment. Otherwise the 'good behavior' clause is a nullity....

"The precedent...asserted by the House in 1804 that a judge may be impeached for a breach of good behavior was reasserted again with full force over one hundred years later in 1912....

"The fact that the House...felt it necessary to make a distinction in the impeachment standards between the Judiciary and the Executive reinforces the obvious —that the words 'treason, bribery, and other high crimes and misdemeanors' are limited solely to indictable crimes and cannot extend to misbehavior....

"The acquittal of President Johnson over a century ago strongly indicates that the Senate has refused to adopt a broad view of 'other high crimes and misdemeanors'.... Impeachment of a President should be resorted to only for cases of the gravest kind—the commission of a crime named in the Constitution or a criminal offense against the laws of the United States. If there is any doubt as to the gravity of an offense or as to a President's conduct or motives, the doubt should be resolved in his favor. This is the necessary price for having an independent executive....

Conclusion: Proper Standard for Presidential Impeachment

"Any analysis that broadly construes the power to impeach and convict can be reached only...by placing a subjective gloss on the history of impeachment that results in permitting the Congress to do whatever it deems most politic. The intent of the Framers, who witnessed episode after episode of outrageous abuse of the impeachment power by the self-righteous English Parliament, was to restrict the *political* reach of the impeachment power.

"Those who seek to broaden the impeachment power invite the use of power 'as a means of crushing political adversaries or ejecting them from office.'.... The acceptance of such an invitation would be destructive to our system of government and to the fundamental principle of separation of powers.... The Framers never intended that the impeachment clause serve to dominate or destroy the executive branch of the government...."

Chiefs

James D. St. Clair, 53, special counsel to the President since Jan. 5, $42,500: a top-ranking Boston trial lawyer with a reputation as a painstakingly thorough preparer of cases and a brilliant courtroom tactician with an almost uncanny recall of details; a member of the Boston firm of Hale & Dorr before he came to the White House; served on the staff of Joseph N. Welch, another member of Hale & Dorr, whose televised clashes with the late Sen. Joseph R. McCarthy (R Wis. 1947-57) as special Army counsel helped end the so-called McCarthy era; a native of Akron, Ohio; a 1941 graduate of the University of Illinois with a law degree from Harvard University, awarded in 1947.

John J. Chester, 53, special counsel to the President since Jan. 30, $40,000: a native of Columbus, Ohio, and a 1942 graduate of Amherst College; law degree from Yale University in 1948. Chester practiced law in Columbus as a partner in the firms of Chester and Chester (1948-57), Chester and Rose (1957-70) and Chester, Hoffman, Park, Willcox and Rose (1970-74). He was elected as a representative to the Ohio General Assembly from Franklin County in 1952, 1954 and 1956.

Also on the White House legal team but not actively involved in the impeachment fight were **J. Fred Buzhardt Jr.,** 50, counsel to the President since Jan. 5, $42,500; and **Leonard Garment,** assistant to the President since Jan. 5, $42,500.

Staff

Cecil Emerson, 39, defense team since Nov. 25, 1973, $32,031: received law degree from Baylor University in 1965; was an assistant district attorney and assistant U.S. attorney in Dallas, Texas, and regional director of the Dallas Drug Enforcement Administration Task Force before coming to the White House.

John A. McCahill, 34; defense team since Nov. 27, 1973, $24,247, paid out of Agriculture Department funds: a 1962 graduate of Columbia, McCahill received a law degree from Catholic University in 1969; was an assistant U.S. attorney in the District of Columbia before joining the White House.

Michael Sterlacci, 31; defense team since Dec. 10, 1973, $24,247, paid out of Transportation Department funds: a 1965 graduate of Seton Hall; received a law degree from George Washington University in 1968; was the assistant general counsel of the United States Information Agency before coming to the White House.

Loren A. Smith, 29, defense team since Nov. 27, 1973, $17,497, paid out of Federal Communications Commission (FCC) funds: a 1966 graduate of Northwestern University; received a law degree from Northwestern in 1969; worked in the general counsel's office of the FCC before joining the White House.

(Continued from p. 37)

Normally, "detailees" would return to their agencies after they had completed their assignments. However, only Smith's salary, $17,497 a year, was being paid by the agency from which he had come.

McCahill and Sterlacci were being paid $24,247 a year each from agencies for which they had never worked: the Departments of Agriculture and Transportation, respectively.

A White House spokesman said the salary arrangements for McCahill and Sterlacci were a matter of "finding a convenient payroll to put them on." The USIA, for which Sterlacci had worked, was not a large enough agency to continue carrying him on its payroll, and McCahill had quit the U.S. attorney's office, according to the White House.

The two other members of St. Clair's team were being paid from White House funds.

St. Clair's associate, John Chester, a 53-year-old Columbus, Ohio, lawyer, was named special counsel to the President on Jan. 30 at a salary of $40,000.

Jerome Murphy, 31, was named a consultant to the President on Dec. 15, 1973, at a fee of $100 a day.

Income Taxes

Absent from the official White House roll of lawyers, but occasionally seen in the Executive Office Building next to the White House, were two prominent tax lawyers: H. Chapman Rose and Kenneth W. Gemmill.

Rose and Gemmill, both former Treasury Department officials during the Eisenhower administration and described by the White House as "old friends of the President," were donating their services to Nixon as consultants in the dispute over Nixon's income tax returns, a White House spokesman told Congressional Quarterly. *(Box, p. 37)*

Defense Strategy. The absence of Rose and Gemmill from government payrolls might have lent weight to what appeared to be shaping up as a key position in Nixon's defense strategy against impeachment. Rep. Wilbur D. Mills (D Ark.), chairman of the Joint Committee on Revenue Taxation, was predicting that his committee's staff study of Nixon's tax returns would increase pressure on Nixon to resign.

The position, some observers predicted, would be that charges of tax evasion were not proper grounds for impeachment since Nixon's tax affairs were not connected with his performance of official duties.

This argument was intimated in a Feb. 28 analysis of the constitutional standard for presidential impeachment, prepared by St. Clair, Chester, Sterlacci, Murphy and Smith.

The analysis contained the following declaration: "The words (in the Constitution) 'Treason, Bribery or other high Crimes and Misdemeanors,' construed either in the light of present day usage or as understood by the framers of the late 18th century, mean what they clearly connote—criminal offenses. Not only do the words inherently require a criminal offense, but one of a very serious nature committed in one's governmental capacity."

WHITE HOUSE, NIXON 1972 CAMPAIGN OFFICIALS INDICTED

(Through March 1974)

Maurice H. Stans, Secretary of Commerce (Jan. 20, 1969 - Feb. 15, 1972); Chairman, Finance Committee for the Reelection of the President (Feb. 15, 1972 - Feb. 11, 1974); Chairman, Republican National Finance Committee (Aug. 23, 1972 - Jan. 17, 1973); indicted May 10, 1973, by a federal grand jury in New York City on charges of conspiracy to obstruct justice, obstruction of justice, and lying to a grand jury; pleaded not guilty on May 21, 1973; trial began Feb. 19, 1974, in U.S. District Court in New York City.

John N. Mitchell, U.S. Attorney General (Jan. 20, 1969 - Feb. 15, 1972); Director, Committee for the Reelection of the President (March 1, 1972 - July 1, 1972); indicted May 10, 1973, by a federal grand jury in New York City on charges of conspiracy to obstruct justice, obstruction of justice by interfering with a federal investigation, and perjury; pleaded not guilty on May 21, 1973; injury for conspiracy to impede the Watergate investigation, obstruction of justice, perjury before the Senate Watergate Committee, and lying to FBI agents and the grand jury; pleaded not guilty on March 9, 1974; trial on the first set of charges began Feb. 19, 1974, in U.S. District Court in New York City; awaiting trial on the second set of charges.

H.R. Haldeman, Assistant to the President (Jan. 20, 1969 - April 30, 1973); indicted March 1, 1974, by the original Watergate grand jury for conspiracy to impede the Watergate investigation, obstruction of justice, and perjury before the Senate Watergate Committee; pleaded not guilty on March 9, 1974; awaiting trial.

Charles W. Colson, Special Counsel to the President (Nov. 6, 1969 - March 10, 1973); indicted March 1, 1974, by the original Watergate grand jury on charges of conspiracy to impede the Watergate investigation and obstruction of justice; pleaded not guilty on March 9, 1974; indicted March 7, 1974, by second Watergate grand jury on charge of conspiracy to violate the constitutional rights of Dr. Lewis Fielding; pleaded not guilty on March 9, 1974; awaiting trial on both sets of charges.

John D. Ehrlichman, Counsel to the President (Jan. 20, 1969 - Nov. 4, 1969); Assistant to the President for Domestic Affairs (Nov. 4, 1969 - April 30, 1973); indicted Sept. 4, 1973, by a Los Angeles County grand jury on charges of burglary, conspiracy and perjury in connection with "plumbers" break-in at the office of Dr. Lewis Fielding; pleaded not guilty on Sept. 7, 1973; indicted March 1, 1974, by the original Watergate grand jury for conspiracy to impede the Watergate investigation, obstruction of justice, and lying to FBI agents and the grand jury; pleaded not guilty on March 9, 1974; indicted March 7, 1974, by the second Watergate grand jury on charges of conspiracy and lying to FBI agents and the grand jury about the "plumbers" break-in to the office of Dr. Lewis Fielding; pleaded not guilty on March 9, 1974; California charges of burglary and conspiracy dropped on March 13, 1974; awaiting trial on state perjury charge; awaiting trial on all federal charges.

John W. Dean III, Associate Deputy Attorney General for Legislation (Jan. 20, 1969 - July 9, 1970); Counsel to the President (July 9, 1970 - April 30, 1973); pleaded guilty on Oct. 19, 1973, to a charge of conspiracy to obstruct justice and defraud the United States; Dean agreed with former special prosecutor Archibald Cox to testify for the prosecution in future trials of White House officials allegedly involved in the Watergate scandal in exchange for immunity from federal prosecution for any other Watergate-related crimes; sentencing was deferred.

Dwight L. Chapin, Deputy Assistant to the President (appointments secretary, Jan. 20, 1969 - Feb. 28, 1973); indicted Nov. 29, 1973, by federal grand jury in Washington on charge of lying to the original Watergate grand jury about his relationship to Donald Segretti; pleaded not guilty on Dec. 7, 1973; awaiting trial.

Egil Krogh Jr., Deputy assistant to the President for Domestic Affairs (May, 1969 - Dec. 9, 1972); Undersecretary of Transportation (Dec., 1972 - May 9, 1973); indicted Sept. 4, 1973, by Los Angeles County grand jury on California counts of burglary and conspiracy involving his role in the break-in of the office of Dr. Lewis Fielding; pleaded not guilty to charges on Sept. 6, 1973; indicted Oct. 11, 1973, by Watergate grand jury for making false statements about burglary of Dr. Fielding's office to former Watergate prosecutor, Earl Silbert; pleaded innocent to charges on Oct. 18, 1973; pleaded guilty Nov. 30, 1973, to violating Dr. Fielding's civil rights, in agreement with Special Prosecutor Leon Jaworski; further federal charges related to the break-in were dropped; California charges dropped on Dec. 3, 1973; sentenced Jan. 24, 1974, to 6 months in prison plus 18 months unsupervised probation; began serving prison term Feb. 4, 1974.

E. Howard Hunt Jr., Consultant to Charles W. Colson, Special Counsel to the President (1970 - April 1, 1972); indicted Sept. 15, 1972, by original Watergate grand jury for conspiracy, burglary, electronic eavesdropping, and wiretapping for his role in the Watergate break-in; pleaded guilty to charges on Jan. 11, 1973; given "provisional" sentence March 23, 1973, by Judge John J. Sirica to be reviewed after a 3 month study; at government's request, granted immunity March 28, 1973, from further prosecution; sentenced Nov. 9, 1973, to 2½ to 8 years in prison and fined $10,000; released Jan. 2, 1974, by order of U.S. Court of Appeals in Washington, while court considered his appeal; asked U.S. Court of Appeals on Feb. 4, 1974, to allow him to change his plea to not guilty, a move previously rejected by Judge Sirica.

G. Gordon Liddy, Special Assistant, Treasury Department (1969-1971); Aide, White House Domestic Counsel (July 20, 1971 - Dec. 10, 1971); General Counsel, Committee for the Re-election of the President (Dec. 1971 - April 1972); Counsel, Finance Committee for the Re-election of the President (April 1972 - June 28, 1972); indicted Sept. 15, 1972, on charges of conspiracy, burglary, electronic eavesdropping and wiretapping for role in Watergate break-in; pleaded not guilty to charges but convicted Jan. 30, 1973; sentenced March 23, 1973, to a minimum sentence of 6 years, 8 months and a maximum sentence of 20 years plus a fine of $40,000; granted immunity March 30, 1973, from further prosecution; found guilty of contempt of court April 3, 1973, for refusal to answer questions before the original Watergate grand jury; sentenced by Judge John J. Sirica to another sentence to last to the end of the term of the grand jury or 18 months, whichever came first; cited July 31, 1973, by House Armed Services Committee for contempt of Congress after his refusal to testify; House passed contempt citation on Sept. 10, 1973; Liddy asked the U.S. Court of Appeals on Aug. 1, 1973, to reverse the contempt citation; indicted Sept. 4, 1973, by Los Angeles County grand jury on California charges of burglary and conspiracy for his role in the break-in of Dr. Lewis Fielding's office; pleaded not guilty to charges on Sept. 20, 1973; asked U.S. Court of Appeals on Oct. 4, 1973, for a new trial, claiming his constitutional rights had been violated by Judge Sirica; indicted March 7, 1974, by second Watergate grand jury for conspiracy to violate the rights of Dr. Fielding and for contempt of Congress; pleaded not guilty to both sets of charges on March 14, 1974; California charges dropped March 13, 1974.

Jeb Stuart Magruder, Special Assistant to the President (Oct. 1, 1969 - Jan. 26, 1970); Deputy Director of Communications, Executive Branch (1970 - May 1, 1971); Staff Director, Citizens for the Re-election of the President (1971-72); Deputy Director, Committee for the Reelection of the President (1972); Executive Director, 1973 Inaugural Committee; Director, Office of Policy Development, Commerce Department (March 13, 1973 - April 26, 1973); pleaded guilty Aug. 16, 1973, to one count of conspiracy to obstruct justice, to unlawfully intercept wire and oral communications and to defraud the U.S. Government; in agreement with Special Prosecutor Archibald Cox, any other potential charges were dropped; sentencing deferred until the completion of future Watergate trials.

Robert C. Mardian, General Counsel, Department of Health, Education and Welfare (1969 - 1970); Assistant Attorney General (1970 - 1972); Political Coordinator, Committee for the Re-election of the President (1972); indicted March 1, 1974, by original Watergate grand jury on charge of conspiracy to impede the Watergate investigation; pleaded not guilty to charge on March 9, 1974; awaiting trial.

Frederick C. LaRue, Special Assistant to the Campaign Director, Committee for the Reelection of the President; pleaded guilty June 27, 1973, in U.S. District Court in Washington to charge of conspiracy to obstruct justice for role in Watergate coverup; sentencing deferred.

Herbert L. Porter, Scheduling Director, Committee for the Re-election of the President; charged Jan. 21, 1974, with lying to FBI agents investigating the Watergate break-in in 1972; Porter waived a formal indictment by a grand jury; pleaded guilty to charge Jan. 28, 1974; sentencing deferred.

Herbert W. Kalmbach, President Nixon's personal attorney; Vice Chairman, Finance Committee for the Re-election of the President (unsalaried position); pleaded guilty Feb. 25, 1974, to charges of helping to run an illegal congressional campaign committee in 1970 and offering an ambassadorial assignment in exchange for a $100,000 campaign contribution; in exchange for plea and offer of cooperation, Special Prosecutor Leon Jaworski

promised not to bring further charges, provided Kalmbach did not commit perjury; sentencing deferred.

Kenneth W. Parkinson, Attorney, Committee for the Re-election of the President; indicted by the original Watergate grand jury for conspiracy to impede the Watergate investigation and obstruction of justice; pleaded not guilty to charges on March 9, 1974; awaiting trial.

Gordon C. Strachan, Staff Assistant to H. R. Haldeman (August 1970 - December 3, 1972); General Counsel, U.S. Information Agency (January 1973 - April 30, 1973); indicted March 1, 1974, by the original Watergate grand jury on charges of conspiracy to impede the Watergate investigation, obstruction of justice, and making false declarations to the grand jury; pleaded not guilty to charges on March 9, 1974; awaiting trial.

James W. McCord Jr., Security Coordinator for the Committee for the Reelection of the President (fired June 18, 1972); indicted Sept. 15, 1972, by original Watergate grand jury on charges of conspiracy, burglary, electronic eavesdropping and wiretapping; pleaded not guilty but convicted January 30, 1973; granted immunity April 5, 1973, from further prosecution; asked for new trial June 8, 1973, on grounds that the government withheld evidence and there was perjury in the first trial; motion denied without hearing Nov. 7, 1973; sentenced Nov. 9, 1973, to 1 to 5 years in prison; asked March 14, 1974, that conviction be vacated on grounds that President Nixon tainted case by failing a year ago to report he had been told hush money was paid to Watergate defendants; sentencing deferred.

David R. Young, Presidential Assistant for the National Security Council (January 5, 1970 - July 1, 1971); Presidential Assistant for Domestic Affairs (July 1, 1971 - April 30, 1973); indicted September 4, 1973, by a Los Angeles County grand jury on charges of burglary and conspiracy for his role in the "plumbers" break-in at the office of Dr. Lewis Fielding; pleaded not guilty to charges on September 7, 1973; California charges dropped on March 13, 1974; granted immunity from federal prosecution on May 16, 1973.

Others Indicted

Also indicted for Watergate-related activities, but not on the payroll of the White House or the Committee for the Re-election of the President, were Donald H. Segretti, George A. Hearing, Bernard L. Barker, Eugenio R. Martinez, Virgilio R. Gonzalez, Frank A. Sturgis, and Felipe De Diego.

Segretti was reportedly recruited for political intelligence activities by Dwight L. Chapin and paid out of funds controlled by Herbert W. Kalmbach. Segretti and his Florida associate, George Hearing, both pleaded guilty to charges of illegal political activity against Democratic Presidential candidates in the 1972 Florida Primary.

Barker, Martinez, Gonzalez and Sturgis pleaded guilty to charges of conspiracy, burglary, electronic eavesdropping and wiretapping, resulting from their involvement in the Watergate break-in. Sturgis and Barker are out of prison while appealing their sentences. Gonzalez and Martinez were scheduled for parole on March 7, 1974.

Barker, Martinez, and Felipe De Diego were indicted March 7, 1974, for their role in breaking into the office of Dr. Lewis Fielding. All three men pleaded not guilty on March 14, 1974, and are awaiting trial.

NIXON SUPPORT IN CONGRESS HITS RECORD LOW IN 1973

President Nixon won 50.6 per cent of the congressional votes on which he took a position during 1973, fewer than any president had won in the 20 years since Congressional Quarterly began measuring presidential support.

Nixon's 1973 support mark was nearly 16 points lower than his 1972 record, and more than 26 points lower than his best score—77 per cent—recorded in 1970. Before 1973, the all-time low was the 52 per cent recorded in 1959, during the Eisenhower administration.

Presidential support actually increased somewhat during the last three months of the year, with both houses taking routine votes on many matters which drew a presidential position but evoked little controversy. This late trend allowed the President to finish the year above the 50 per cent mark, but did not erase the all-time record low.

The study was based on 310 votes that featured a .clear-cut presidential position. There were more such votes in 1973 than in any other year in the history of the study, but this was due mainly to an increase in the total number of votes cast. The President took a position on 27 per cent of the votes during the year, well above the 10 per cent he recorded in 1972 but far below the 20-year average of 45 per cent.

Votes were included in the 1973 study only if the President or his aides had made a specific indication of his wishes before the vote was taken.

The two chambers of Congress were about equal in their support of the President during the year, with the Senate backing Nixon 52 per cent of the time, and the House 48 per cent. This was a marked contrast with 1972, when Senate support was 54 per cent but House support was 81 per cent. It was the first time since 1969, Nixon's first year in office, that the Senate supported him more often than the House.

More Than Watergate

In conversations with Congressional Quarterly, members of both houses said the Watergate affair was not the most important reason for the decline in presidential support during 1973. They attributed much of the change to the President's threats in the beginning of the year to dismantle long-standing social programs.

"They cut off disaster aid and rural environmental assistance and rural water-sewer funds," recalled Rep. John M. Zwach (R Minn.). "These were things we were naturally not going to go along with."

Congress sustained the President's vetoes on most of these economic issues, but it expressed its anger by reducing its over-all support score to 43 per cent during the first seven months of the year. Never before had a President lost more support tests in Congress than he had won.

Until U.S. bombing of Cambodia ended in August, the Indochina war had an effect on presidential support in Congress. "One of the major thorns this year was the war," admitted White House lobbyist Max Friedersdorf, "and this was poisoning our whole effort with Congress."

Congressional and White House sources differed on why the President's legislative requests fared better during the last part of the year. "When the White House got in trouble over Watergate," argued Sen. Robert T. Stafford (R Vt.), "they began to work and compromise."

Rep. H. John Heinz III (R Pa.) said the same thing was happening in the House. "The White House wasn't looking for an argument that they would lose," Heinz said. He mentioned compromises on a manpower bill, a health maintenance organization bill, and a northeast railroad bill.

But Friedersdorf said it was Congress that was learning to compromise. "When the House sustained the vetoes," he said, "this had a sobering effect on the Democratic leadership. We could sense the frustration that they felt when they could not win on these issues. This had an effect and helped us."

Others pointed out that the end of the year gave both houses a chance to vote on numerous issues where there was little disagreement, and offered some easy padding for the President's support score.

"Right at the end of the year," said Sen. Richard S. Schweiker (R Pa.), "there were a lot of nominations and the energy thing. We're all for measures to help save energy."

The year-end increase in presidential support also was related to a large number of non-controversial Senate votes on treaties, most of which came after the August recess. Had treaty votes been excluded from the study, the President's support score both for the Senate and for Congress would have been 48 per cent. Nearly all the treaties were approved unanimously.

Support Breakdown

Party Differences. In both chambers, the average Democrat opposed the President a majority of the time. Composite scores show that Democrats in the Senate voted against the President 51 per cent of the time and supported him 37 per cent. This was a switch from 1972, when the average Senate Democrat supported the President more often (44 per cent) than he opposed him (41 per cent). House Democrats showed a similar trend.

The average Republican in both the House and the Senate supported the President nearly two-thirds of the time: 61 per cent in the Senate and 62 per cent in the House. The 1973 Republican scores reflected a slight drop in support from 1972 in both chambers.

State and Regional Averages. As in previous years, southerners were more likely to go along with the President's wishes than those in any other regional bloc. This was true in both parties. The average southern Senate Republican backed the President 69 per cent of the time, while his Democratic counterpart supported Nixon 47 per cent of the time. Southern Republicans in the Senate supported the President more often than members from any other region in either party.

In the Senate, the leading opponents of the President were midwestern Democrats (30 per cent). In the House, that distinction went to Democrats from the East (29 per cent). Among Republicans, easterners were the least frequent Nixon supporters in both chambers (53 per cent in the Senate and 58 per cent in the House).

Members from the East and Far West, Republicans as well as Democrats, supported the President less often in 1973 than in 1972. Republican House members from the South and Midwest, and Democratic senators from the Midwest, all averaged higher over-all in presidential support than they had the previous year.

Senators and representatives from Nebraska had the highest support average of any state delegation in Congress, supporting the President 71 per cent of the time, while opposing him 24 per cent. The Massachusetts delegation was the least supportive, with a support score of 33 per cent and an opposition score of 61. Nebraska's five-member delegation is all Republican; Massachusetts has 10 Democrats and four Republicans.

Individual Scorers. The strongest Nixon supporter in the Senate was Clifford P. Hansen (R Wyo.), who scored 78 per cent. Next came 15 other Republicans, led by party whip Robert P. Griffin (Mich.) with 77 per cent; Jesse A. Helms (N.C.), Dewey F. Bartlett (Okla.), and Strom Thurmond (S.C.), all with 76 per cent; and Paul J. Fannin (Ariz.), Roman L. Hruska (Neb.) and John G. Tower (Texas), all with 75 per cent.

The leading Democratic supporters of the President in the Senate were all southerners. First was James B. Allen (Ala.), who had a 66 per cent score. Behind him were John L. McClellan (Ark.) and Sam Nunn (Ga.) with 56 per cent; and John Sparkman (Ala.) and James O. Eastland (Miss.) with 55. Independent Harry F. Byrd (Va.) had a support score of 63 per cent.

In the House, the Republican leadership ranked at the top in presidential support. First was Barber B. Conable (N.Y.), chairman of the House Republican Policy Committee. He voted with Nixon 86 per cent of the time.

After Conable came Gerald R. Ford (Mich.), who was House minority leader until he was confirmed as Vice President Dec. 6. Ford had an 80 per cent support score. Next came Leslie C. Arends (Ill.), the minority whip, and Samuel L. Devine (Ohio), vice-chairman of the party conference. Both scored 79.

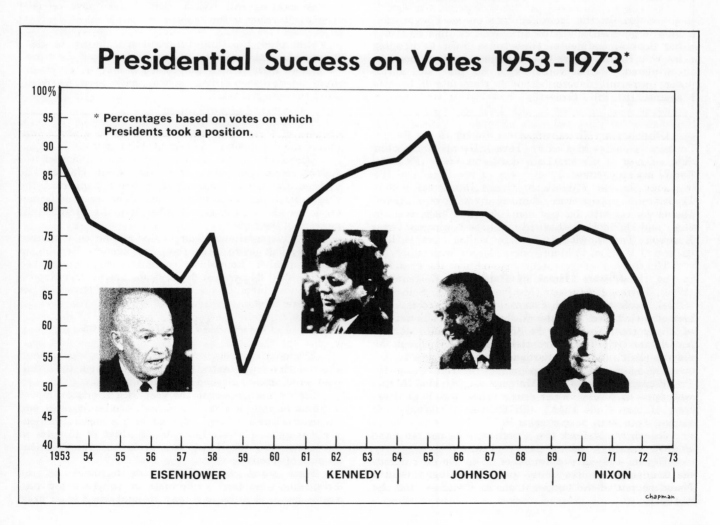

Presidential Success on Votes 1953-1973*

* Percentages based on votes on which Presidents took a position.

EISENHOWER   KENNEDY   JOHNSON   NIXON

chapman

Ground Rules for CQ Presidential Support-Opposition

• **Presidential Issues**—CQ analyzes all messages, press conference remarks and other public statements of the President to determine what he personally, as distinct from other administration spokesmen, does or does not want in the way of legislative action.

• **Borderline Cases**—By the time an issue reaches a vote, it may differ from the original form on which the President expressed himself. In such cases, CQ analyzes the measure to determine whether, on balance, the features favored by the President outweigh those he opposed or vice versa. Only then is the vote classified.

• **Some Votes Excluded**—Occasionally, important measures are so extensively amended on the floor that it is impossible to characterize final passage as a victory or defeat for the President.

• **Motions**—Votes on motions to recommit, to reconsider or to table often are key tests that govern the legislative outcome. Such votes are necessarily included in the Nixon support tabulations.

• **Rules**—In the House, debate on most significant bills is governed by rules that restrict time and may bar floor amendments. These rules must be adopted by the House before the bills in question may be considered. Members may vote for the rule, in order to permit debate, although they intend to vote against the bill. Generally, however, a vote against

a rule is a vote against the bill, and vice versa, since rejection of the rule prevents consideration of the bill. CQ assumes that if the President favored a bill, he favored the rule unless it was a closed rule that would prevent amendments he wanted.

• **Appropriations**—Generally, votes on passage of appropriation bills are not included in the tabulation, since it is rarely possible to determine the President's position on the over-all revisions Congress almost invariably makes in the sums allowed. Votes to cut or increase specific funds requested in the President's budget, however, are included.

• **Failures to Vote**—In tabulating the Support or Opposition scores of members on the selected Nixon-issue votes, CQ counts only "yea" and "nay" votes on the ground that only these affect the outcome. Most failures to vote reflect absences because of illness or official business. Failures to vote lower both support and opposition scores equally.

• **Weighting**—All Nixon-issue votes have equal statistical weight in the analysis.

• **Changed Position**—Presidential Support is determined by the position of the President at the time of a vote even though that position may be different from an earlier position, or may have been reversed after the vote was taken.

Other strong Nixon supporters among House Republicans were James M. Collins (Texas), George A. Goodling (Pa.), David C. Treen (La.) and John Ware (Pa.). All had 77 per cent scores.

John Jarman (Okla.) led House Democrats with a 72 per cent support score. Runners-up were W. C. (Dan) Daniel (Va.), with 66 per cent; Joe D. Waggonner Jr. (La.) and David E. Satterfield (Va.), both with 65; Omar Burleson (Texas), with 64; George Mahon (Texas), with 62; and G. V. (Sonny) Montgomery (Miss.), with 60.

The three most consistent opponents of the President in the House were Democrats Robert W. Kastenmeier (Wis.), Parren J. Mitchell (Md.) and John F. Seiberling (Ohio), each with 73 per cent opposition scores. Five Democrats shared the second highest opposition score of 72 per cent. They were Phillip Burton (Calif.), Ronald V. Dellums (Calif.), Henry Helstoski (N.J.), Joseph M. Gaydos (Pa.) and Paul S. Sarbanes (Md.).

The most persistent opponent in the House from the President's own party was Margaret M. Heckler (Mass.) who opposed Nixon 57 per cent of the time. Behind her were Gilbert Gude (Md.) and Charles W. Whalen Jr. (Ohio), both with 55 per cent; Robert H. Steele (Conn.) and Joseph M. McDade (Pa.), both with 54 per cent; and Paul W. Cronin (Mass.), with 53 per cent.

House Judiciary Committee. The House committee studying the possibility of impeaching President Nixon supported the President about as often as the rest of the House. The average support score for the committee was 45.7 per cent, while the House as a whole supported the President 47 per cent of the time in 1973.

Democrats on the Judiciary Committee showed less support than Democrats from the whole House. The average Democratic committee member supported the President 31 per cent of the time. The average Democratic member of the House sided with the President 35 per cent of the time.

The average Republican on the committee supported the President more often than the average Republican House member. Republican committee members backed the President 64 per cent of the time. The average Republican House member sided with President Nixon 62 per cent of the time.

Nixon's Wins and Losses

Economic controls, rural programs, energy policy and the Indochina war were the issues over which the President and Congress clashed most often in 1973.

Both chambers began the year with efforts to impose a freeze or roll-back on prices, rents, interest rates and dividends. The President opposed such a move. The Senate was able to defeat him on only three of 13 votes in this area, while the House went along with the President on each of seven occasions.

Farm issues were another battleground, as the President attempted to eliminate or cut back aid programs for rural areas and tried to hold the line on price

State Averages

Following are 1973 presidential support and opposition scores for each state delegation. Ranking is according to combined chambers' support score, carried to the necessary decimal places to break a tie.

	Rank	Both Chambers		Senate		House	
		Support	Opposition	Support	Opposition	Support	Opposition
Total							
Congress		47	43	47	41	47	44
South		52	38	55	32	52	40
Midwest		48	42	41	46	50	41
West		45	44	46	41	44	46
East		42	49	45	45	42	50
Ala.	7	58	33	60	32	56	34
Alaska	29	46	42	42	42	57	39
Ariz.	3	60	23	60	12	61	31
Ark.	38	41	41	41	42	41	40
Calif.	36	43	46	31	56	43	45
Colo.	22	49	44	49	41	49	46
Conn.	39	41	54	44	49	39	56
Del.	15	52	38	50	47	57	41
Fla.	21	49	43	51	40	48	44
Ga.	28	47	44	53	41	45	45
Hawaii	42	40	51	47	41	31	67
Idaho	14	52	38	45	42	63	31
Ill.	18	50	40	40	48	51	39
Ind.	17	51	40	28	56	57	38
Iowa	37	42	49	25	54	49	47
Kan.	4	59	32	56	32	61	32
Ky.	33	44	49	43	47	45	49
La.	25	48	39	42	43	50	38
Maine	49	33	59	28	61	40	57
Md.	24	49	47	55	36	46	52
Mass.	50	33	61	35	53	32	63
Mich.	20	50	39	51	47	50	39
Minn.	41	41	49	29	59	45	46
Miss.	12	53	27	38	16	62	34
Mo.	44	37	55	33	56	38	54
Mont.	46	35	57	31	63	42	48
Neb.	1	71	24	74	19	67	30
Nev.	31	45	46	41	51	57	34
N. H.	11	55	33	49	34	65	32
N. J.	40	41	51	36	55	42	50
N. M.	19	50	43	52	44	46	42
N. Y.	35	43	44	54	27	42	45
N. C.	9	57	38	64	27	55	41
N. D.	26	48	49	48	50	46	46
Ohio	13	52	37	58	18	51	39
Okla.	5	59	31	71	22	52	36
Ore.	23	49	38	51	37	47	39
Penn.	32	45	48	53	42	44	49
R. I.	48	35	58	41	53	24	65
S. C.	6	58	34	59	32	58	35
S. D.	47	35	53	25	60	49	42
Tenn.	10	57	33	63	20	54	38
Texas	27	47	42	60	30	46	44
Utah	30	45	40	50	34	37	50
Vt.	8	57	37	54	39	66	32
Va.	2	68	28	68	26	68	29
Wash.	45	36	56	43	50	33	59
W. Va.	43	37	59	41	56	34	60
Wis.	34	44	52	36	62	47	49
Wyo.	16	52	37	60	27	28	68

supports in the 1973 Agriculture Act. Both chambers delivered 12 defeats to the President on farm and rural issues. The President had only four victories in the Senate and six in the House.

The year-end rush to pass energy legislation left the President with mixed results. Both chambers defeated the President in passing fuel allocation bills, but supported his efforts to establish year-round daylight saving time and reorganize energy research and development.

Each chamber made six attempts to override presidential vetoes. The Senate voted to override three times, but twice the House chose to sustain. The only veto the House voted to override, and the only veto actually overridden in 1973, came on the bill limiting a president's warmaking powers.

Congressional attempts to end all American combat involvement in the Indochina war provided a substantial number of defeats for the President. The House went against Nixon on nine of eleven votes in its effort to cut off funds for American bombing of Cambodia.

Average Scores

Following are composites of Republican and Democratic scores for 1973, compared with those for 1972.

	1973		1972	
	Dem.	Rep.	Dem.	Rep.
SUPPORT				
Senate	37%	61%	44%	66%
House	35	62	47	64
OPPOSITION				
Senate	51	27	41	20
House	55	30	37	22

Regional Averages

SUPPORT

Regional presidential support scores for 1973; scores for 1972 are in parentheses:

DEMOCRATS

	East	West	South	Midwest
Senate	35% (36%)	35% (40%)	47% (60%)	30% (29%)
House	29 (48)	30 (44)	45 (48)	31 (45)

REPUBLICANS

	East	West	South	Midwest
Senate	53% (63%)	62% (66%)	69% (73%)	62% (64%)
House	58 (70)	61 (63)	66 (58)	65 (63)

OPPOSITION

Regional presidential opposition scores for 1973; scores for 1972 are in parentheses:

DEMOCRATS

	East	West	South	Midwest
Senate	56% (45%)	55% (42%)	39% (25%)	59% (57%)
House	62 (39)	60 (39)	46 (33)	60 (40)

Republicans	East	West	South	Midwest
Senate	36% (30%)	23% (16%)	22% (11%)	25% (16%)
House	35 (19)	30 (17)	27 (28)	28 (23)

High Scorers—Support

Highest individual scorers in Nixon support—those who voted for the President's position most often in 1973.

SENATE

Democrats		Republicans	
Allen (Ala.)	66%	Hansen (Wyo.)	78%
Byrd (Va.)†	63	Griffin (Mich.)	77
McClellan (Ark.)	56	Helms (N.C.)	76
Nunn (Ga.)	56	Bartlett (Okla.)	76
Sparkman (Ala.)	55	Thurmond (S.C.)	76
Eastland (Miss.)	55	Fannin (Ariz.)	75
		Hruska (Neb.)	75
† *Elected as independent*		Tower (Texas)	75
		Curtis (Neb.)	72
		Scott (Va.)	72

HOUSE

Democrats		Republicans	
Jarman (Okla.)	72%	Conable (N.Y.)	86%
Daniel (Va.)	66	Ford (Mich.)	80*
Waggonner (La.)	65	Arends (Ill.)	79
Satterfield (Va.)	65	Devine (Ohio)	79
Burleson (Texas)	64	Treen (La.)	77
Mahon (Texas)	62	Ware (Pa.)	77*
Montgomery (Miss.)	60	Goodling (Pa.)	77*
Haley (Fla.)	59	Collins (Texas)	77
Whitten (Miss.)	59	Rhodes (Ariz.)	76
Mann (S.C.)	59	Dennis (Ind.)	76
Sikes (Fla.)	58	Cederberg (Mich.)	76
Bowen (Miss.)	58	Schneebeli (Pa.)	76*
Casey (Texas)	58	Martin (Neb.)	76

Not eligible for all recorded votes in 1973.

High-Scorers—Opposition

Highest individual scorers in Nixon opposition—those who voted against the President's position most often in 1973.

SENATE

Democrats		Republicans	
Hathaway (Maine)	68%	Case (N.J.)	57%
Nelson (Wis.)	66	Schweiker (Pa.)	57
Mansfield (Mont.)	64	Brooke (Mass.)	48
McGovern (S.D.)	64	Hatfield (Ore.)	46
Burdick (N.D.)	63	Mathias (Md.)	42
Metcalf (Mont.)	62	Stafford (Vt.)	41
Stevenson (Ill.)	61	Weicker (Conn.)	40
Hartke (Ind.)	60	Javits (N.Y.)	39
Byrd (W.Va.)	60	Pearson (Kan.)	38

HOUSE

Democrats		Republicans	
Mitchell (Md.)	73%	Heckler (Mass.)	57%
Seiberling (Ohio)	73	Gude (Md.)	55
Kastenmeier (Wis.)	73	Whalen (Ohio)	55
Burton (Calif.)	72	Steele (Conn.)	54
Dellums (Calif.)	72	McDade (Pa.)	54
Sarbanes (Md.)	72	Cronin (Mass.)	53
Helstoski (N.J.)	72	Biester (Pa.)	52
Gaydos (Pa.)	72	Rinaldo (N.J.)	51

1973 Nixon Issue Votes

Following is a list of all Senate and House recorded votes between Jan. 3 and Dec. 22, 1973, on which the President took a position. The votes, listed by CQ vote number, appear in the roll call chart section of the *1973 Congressional Quarterly Almanac.*

SENATE VOTES (185)

Presidential Victories (97)—1, 2, 3, 4, 14, 34, 44, 46, 48, 49, 50, 52, 56, 57, 58, 59, 60, 64, 69, 70, 72, 74, 100, 118, 136, 141, 145, 164, 165, 180, 221, 228, 234, 235, 236, 239, 240, 243, 251, 252, 253, 254, 275, 289, 315, 352, 359, 360, 361, 362, 363, 364, 366, 375, 383, 392, 394, 396, 397, 400, 407, 410, 412, 413, 415, 416, 417, 418, 425, 427, 428, 429, 430, 431, 432, 435, 455, 456, 457, 458, 459, 463, 470, 493, 495, 496, 499, 508, 527, 530, 532, 536, 568, 580, 582, 586, 587.

Presidential Defeats (88)—5, 6, 8, 9, 16, 20, 21, 24, 26, 29, 31, 32, 36, 37, 45, 55, 65, 66, 79, 84, 85, 87, 98, 111, 112, 113, 114, 117, 121, 126, 127, 144, 154, 162, 163, 166, 167, 168, 169, 170, 171, 188, 191, 209, 210, 211, 218, 219, 224, 230, 231, 232, 233, 237, 238, 241, 242, 255, 258, 259, 267, 268, 291, 299, 303, 346, 254, 355, 356, 357, 358, 372, 373, 376, 409, 421, 422, 426, 451, 462, 465, 525, 528, 531, 551, 552, 553, 577.

HOUSE VOTES (125)

Presidential Victories (60)—15, 38, 39, 46, 52, 54, 55, 56, 57, 59, 68, 79, 85, 93, 95, 96, 103, 110, 118, 123, 131, 147, 148, 150, 155, 173, 190, 212, 215, 220, 221, 224, 226, 230, 233, 250, 257, 272, 302, 306, 325, 328, 329, 336, 341, 364, 409, 421, 437, 441, 442, 468, 472, 475, 477, 479, 480, 489, 525, 531.

Presidential Defeats (65)—10, 13, 19, 25, 26, 30, 41, 42, 66, 71, 73, 87, 88, 89, 90, 91, 94, 112, 119, 120, 121, 122, 124, 125, 127, 129, 134, 157, 172, 189, 192, 198, 199, 200, 201, 218, 225, 227, 228, 229, 231, 232, 241, 249, 258, 259, 277, 310, 366, 367, 382, 395, 402, 404, 407, 412, 417, 418, 420, 425, 444, 463, 471, 473, 474.

	1	2	3	4
ALABAMA				
Allen	66	33	66	31
Sparkman	55	31	59	16
ALASKA				
Gravel	26	51	20	54
Stevens	57	34	54	31
ARIZONA				
Fannin	75	14	81	12
Goldwater	45	9	56	9
ARKANSAS				
Fulbright	26	47	29	59
McClellan	56	38	53	34
CALIFORNIA				
Cranston	32	56	35	60
Tunney	30	56	37	52
COLORADO				
Haskell	32	56	—	—
Dominick	65	25	67	9
CONNECTICUT				
Ribicoff	37	57	32	56
Weicker	51	40	66	21
DELAWARE				
Biden	30	49	—	—
Roth	71	25	84	16
FLORIDA				
Chiles	39	52	51	40
Gurney	64	28	86	13
GEORGIA				
Nunn	56	40	—	—
Talmadge	50	43	61	34
HAWAII				
Inouye	32	56	31	47
Fong	61	26	71	12
IDAHO				
Church	28	59	31	55
McClure	61	24	—	—
ILLINOIS				
Stevenson	34	61	37	55
Percy	45	36	48	37
INDIANA				
Bayh	30	53	25	50
Hartke	27	60	20	41

	1	2	3	4
IOWA				
Clark	26	50	—	—
Hughes	24	57	29	63
KANSAS				
Dole	71	27	83	10
Pearson	41	38	57	32
KENTUCKY				
Huddleston	30	58	—	—
Cook	56	37	56	28
LOUISIANA				
Johnston	46	38	—	—
Long	48	47	59	23
MAINE				
Hathaway	30	68	—	—
Muskie	26	54	19	42
MARYLAND				
Beall	68	30	77	17
Mathias	43	42	43	44
MASSACHUSETTS				
Kennedy	30	58	27	51
Brooke	39	48	44	48
MICHIGAN				
Hart	24	59	32	59
Griffin	77	15	84	8
MINNESOTA				
Humphrey	34	59	32	45
Mondale	25	58	33	63
MISSISSIPPI				
Eastland	55	31	65	16
Stennis	22	2	72	24
MISSOURI				
Eagleton	33	58	37	52
Symington	33	55	40	56
MONTANA				
Mansfield	29	64	30	55
Metcalf	36	62	26	46
NEBRASKA				
Curtis	72	18	70	13
Hruska	75	19	84	10
NEVADA				
Bible	39	53	54	34
Cannon	42	48	55	26

	1	2	3	4
NEW HAMPSHIRE				
McIntyre	40	55	42	37
Cotton	58	14	74	14
NEW JERSEY				
Williams	29	54	32	59
Case	42	57	44	50
NEW MEXICO				
Montoya	38	59	41	49
Domenici	67	28	—	—
NEW YORK				
*Buckley**	70†	14†	78	13
Javits	38	39	46	39
NORTH CAROLINA				
Ervin	53	34	65	28
Helms	76	21	—	—
NORTH DAKOTA				
Burdick	34	63	35	58
Young	63	36	72	19
OHIO				
Saxbe	58†	19†	63	14
Taft	58	17	70*	13*
OKLAHOMA				
Bartlett	76	22	—	—
Bellmon	65	23	70	10
OREGON				
Hatfield	45	46	27	50
Packwood	57	28	63	18
PENNSYLVANIA				
Schweiker	42	57	50	48
Scott	64	26	75	9
RHODE ISLAND				
Pastore	42	50	43	49
Pell	41	56	31	48
SOUTH CAROLINA				
Hollings	43	49	48	31
Thurmond	76	16	77	16
SOUTH DAKOTA				
Abourezk	25	58	—	—
McGovern	25	64	12	39
TENNESSEE				
Baker	57	25	66	13
Brock	68	16	71	13

- KEY -

† Not eligible for all roll calls in 1973.

* Not eligible for all roll calls in 92nd Congress.

	1	2	3	4
TEXAS				
Bentsen	44	47	59	36
Tower	75	14	70	9
UTAH				
Moss	30	58	30	49
Bennett	70	9	69	12
VERMONT				
Aiken	57	37	66	26
Stafford	51	41	49*	35*
VIRGINIA				
Byrd, Jr.**	63	33	72	26
Scott	72	20	—	—
WASHINGTON				
Jackson	47	53	48	20
Magnuson	38	47	39	40
WEST VIRGINIA				
Byrd	40	60	59	34
Randolph	42	53	46	44
WISCONSIN				
Nelson	31	66	29	66
Proxmire	41	59	38	62
WYOMING				
McGee	42	39	56	17
Hansen	78	14	70	13

Democrats   *Republicans*   *Buckley elected as Conservative*   **Byrd elected as independent*

Presidential Support and Opposition: Senate

1. Support Score, 1973. Percentage of 185 Nixon-issue roll calls in 1973 on which senator voted "yea" or "nay" *in agreement* with the President's position. Failures to vote lower both Support and Opposition scores.

2. Opposition Score, 1973. Percentage of 185 Nixon-issue roll calls in 1973 on which senator voted "yea" or "nay" *in disagreement* with the President's position. Failures to vote lower both Support and Opposition scores.

3. Support Score, 92nd Congress. Percentage of 128 Nixon-issue roll calls in 1971 and 1972 on which senator voted "yea" or "nay" *in agreement* with the President's position. Failures to vote lower both Support and Opposition scores.

4. Opposition Score, 92nd Congress. Percentage of 128 Nixon-issue roll calls in 1971 and 1972 on which senator voted "yea" or "nay" *in disagreement* with the President's position. Failures to vote lower both Support and Opposition scores.

Presidential Support
And Opposition: House

1. Support Score, 1973. Percentage of 125 Nixon-issue roll calls in 1973 on which representative voted "yea" or "nay" *in agreement* with the President's position. Failures to vote lower both Support and Opposition scores.

2. Opposition Score, 1973. Percentage of 125 Nixon-issue roll calls in 1973 on which representative voted "yea" or "nay" *in disagreement* with the President's position. Failures to vote lower both Support and Opposition scores.

3. Support Score, 92nd Congress. Percentage of 94 Nixon-issue roll calls in 1971 and 1972 on which representative voted "yea" or "nay" *in agreement* with the President's position. Failures to vote lower both Support and Opposition scores.

4. Opposition Score, 92nd Congress. Percentage of 94 Nixon-issue roll calls in 1971 and 1972 on which representative voted "yea" or "nay" *in disagreement* with the President's position. Failures to vote lower both Support and Opposition scores.

1 *Rep. Donald Young (R Alaska) sworn in March 14, 1973, to replace Rep. Nick Begich (D), deceased.*

2 *Rep. Cardiss Collins (D Ill.) sworn in June 7, 1973, to replace Rep. George W. Collins (D), deceased.*

3 *Rep. Corinne C. Boggs (D La.) sworn in March 27, 1973, to replace Rep. Hale Boggs (D), deceased.*

4 *Rep. William O. Mills (R Md.) died May 24, 1973. His scores for 1973 were 68 per cent support and 32 per cent opposition. Rep. Robert E. Bauman (R Md.) sworn in Sept. 5, 1973, to replace Mills.*

5 *Rep. Gerald R. Ford (R Mich.) resigned Dec. 6, 1973, to become Vice President.*

6 *Rep. Donald W. Riegle (D Mich.) switched to the Democratic party on Feb. 27, 1973. The 92nd Congress scores reflect Riegle as a Republican. His scores for 1973 as a Republican were 0 per cent support and 66 per cent opposition.*

7 *Rep. Carl Albert (D Okla.), as Speaker, votes at his own discretion.*

8 *Rep. John P. Saylor (R Pa.) died Oct. 28, 1973.*

- KEY -

†Not eligible for all recorded votes in 1973.

*Not eligible for all recorded votes in 92nd Congress.

—Not a member of 92nd Congress.

	1	2	3	4
ALABAMA				
1 Edwards	73	23	69	17
2 Dickinson	70	22	62	21
3 Nichols	52	38	53	20
4 Bevill	46	50	61	24
5 Jones	39	39	57	31
6 Buchanan	64	24	82	14
7 Flowers	50	40	69	19
ALASKA				
AL Young[1]	57†	39†	—	—
ARIZONA				
1 Rhodes	76	16	81	9
2 Udall	38	57	31	54
3 Steiger	62	25	59	24
4 Conlan	67	26	—	—
ARKANSAS				
1 Alexander	33	53	43	34
2 Mills	26	25	57	23
3 Hammer-schmidt	62	32	73	23
4 Thornton	45	52	—	—
CALIFORNIA				
1 Clausen	52	39	80	16
2 Johnson	28	61	66	30
3 Moss	30	63	32	49
4 Leggett	30	58	41	45
5 Burton	25	72	30	66
6 Mailliard	56	28	83	9
7 Dellums	23	72	28	64
8 Stark	24	71	—	—
9 Edwards	21	70	35	63
10 Gubser	61	22	70	3
11 Ryan	25	53	—	—
12 Talcott	62	24	73	14
13 Teague	66†	31†	87	9
14 Waldie	20	58	31	50
15 McFall	42	50	65	28
16 Sisk	37	56	55	34
17 McCloskey	45	48	47	35
18 Mathias	58	34	70	11
19 Holifield	37	56	56	29
20 Moorhead	70	22	—	—
21 Hawkins	20	63	32	45
22 Corman	31	63	36	46
23 Clawson	63	21	60	18
24 Rousselot	58	34	46	32
25 Wiggins	64	13	76	9
26 Rees	30	64	34	54
27 Goldwater	71	19	63	17
28 Bell	40†	35†	62	10
29 Danielson	22	47	50	46
30 Roybal	26	67	32	60
31 Wilson	30	66	49	28
32 Hosmer	70	20	85	5
33 Pettis	61	29	79	13
34 Hanna	28	46	48	30
35 Anderson	30	64	46	47
36 Ketchum	65	26	—	—
37 Burke	15	51	—	—
38 Brown	30	61	—	—
39 Hinshaw	69	26	—	—
40 Wilson	65	23	74	9
41 Van Deerlin	34	62	43	44
42 Burgener	67	25	—	—
43 Veysey	59	20	74	12
COLORADO				
1 Schroeder	29	71	—	—
2 Brotzman	62	34	82	14
3 Evans	38	58	35	46
4 Johnson	43	46	—	—
5 Armstrong	74	23	—	—

	1	2	3	4
CONNECTICUT				
1 Cotter	29	65	48	43
2 Steele	43	54	60	26
3 Giaimo	32	59	49	31
4 McKinney	47	45	63	23
5 Sarasin	53	47	—	—
6 Grasso	31	66	44	38
DELAWARE				
AL DuPont	57	41	78	19
FLORIDA				
1 Sikes	58	33	59	24
2 Fuqua	41	39	59	30
3 Bennett	43	57	54	46
4 Chappell	53	39	59	29
5 Gunter	41	50	—	—
6 Young	63	31	74	22
7 Gibbons	38	53	47	45
8 Haley	59	40	56	34
9 Frey	66	22	71	16
10 Bafalis	66	28	—	—
11 Rogers	50	50	65	33
12 Burke	60	29	62	23
13 Lehman	29	63	—	—
14 Pepper	28	59	63	30
15 Fascell	31	64	53	41
GEORGIA				
1 Ginn	41	58	—	—
2 Mathis	48	42	63	33
3 Brinkley	54	46	65	34
4 Blackburn	62	19	59	22
5 Young	26	71	—	—
6 Flynt	45	44	43	26
7 Davis	43	46	63	20
8 Stuckey	45	50	38	30
9 Landrum	37	36	51	24
10 Stephens	50	42	65	21
HAWAII				
1 Matsunaga	33	63	41	47
2 Mink	29	70	34	60
IDAHO				
1 Symms	58	34	—	—
2 Hansen	69	28	80	6
ILLINOIS				
1 Metcalfe	25	58	30	34
2 Murphy, M.	31	60	45	40
3 Hanrahan	68	29	—	—
4 Derwinski	59	22	51	15
5 Kluczynski	33	53	55	28
6 Collier	66	22	74	15
7 Collins[2]	24	63	—	—
8 Rostenkowski	26	57	51	33
9 Yates	37	62	36	62
10 Young	70	22	—	—
11 Annunzio	32	66	52	33
12 Crane	60	26	50	38
13 McClory	67	27	74	16
14 Erlenborn	67	17	79	6
15 Arends	79	16	82	6
16 Anderson	55	29	84	9
17 O'Brien	71	21	—	—
18 Michel	75	17	66	19
19 Railsback	51†	35†	65	18
20 Findley	58	39	67	16
21 Madigan	69	30	—	—
22 Shipley	34	59	50	37
23 Price	33	66	71	24
24 Gray	26	49	54	33
INDIANA				
1 Madden	34	62	43	53
2 Landgrebe	63	22	62	33
3 Brademas	28	69	38	57
4 Roush	36	58	38	57
5 Hillis	61	32	81	9
6 Bray	72	22	74	18
7 Myers	71	21	71	26
8 Zion	70	22	77	17
9 Hamilton	41	58	52	45
10 Dennis	76	23	67	28
11 Hudnut	72	25	—	—
IOWA				
1 Mezvinsky	34	66	—	—
2 Culver	34	61	32	55
3 Gross	55	40	43	46
4 Smith	38	58	43	48

Democrats   *Republicans*

	1	2	3	4
5 Scherle	65	31	56	33
6 Mayne	70	25	72	18
KANSAS				
1 Sebelius	71	26	73	19
2 Roy	40	54	36	60
3 Winn	66	26	78	13
4 Shriver	69	26	83	17
5 Skubitz	61	30	70	16
KENTUCKY				
1 Stubblefield	48	46	56	32
2 Natcher	39	61	60	40
3 Mazzoli	45	54	46	53
4 Snyder	54	44	50	44
5 Carter	44	30	74	15
6 Breckinridge	49	48	—	—
7 Perkins	38	62	54	44
LOUISIANA				
1 Hebert	35	25	47	7
2 Boggs[3]	40†	56†	—	—
3 Treen	77	21	—	—
4 Waggonner	65	31	66	23
5 Passman	54	34	54	24
6 Rarick	51	42	46	43
7 Breaux	37	45	60*	20*
8 Long, G.	42	54	—	—
MAINE				
1 Kyros	27	68	37	55
2 Cohen	53	46	—	—
MARYLAND				
1 Bauman[4]	54†	46†	—	—
2 Long	30	68	32	65
3 Sarbanes	28	72	38	57
4 Holt	69	30	—	—
5 Hogan	67	31	80	17
6 Byron	57	42	77	20
7 Mitchell	22	73	30	62
8 Gude	40	55	47	48
MASSACHUSETTS				
1 Conte	43	49	51	41
2 Boland	36	62	52	45
3 Donohue	28	67	29	44
4 Drinan	33	67	38	62
5 Cronin	37	53	—	—
6 Harrington	29	62	43	56
7 Macdonald	23	66	37	48
8 O'Neill	31	63	47	46
9 Moakley	27	71	—	—
10 Heckler	38	57	44	40
11 Burke	29	70	46	54
12 Studds	30	70	—	—
MICHIGAN				
1 Conyers	20	50	28	54
2 Esch	56	31	50	30
3 Brown	71	25	81	16
4 Hutchinson	75	25	65	33
5 Ford[5]	80†	16†	82	7
6 Chamberlain	72	24	85	11
7 Riegle[6]	25	62	34	47
8 Harvey	50	26	66	26
9 Vander Jagt	58	30	68	18
10 Cederberg	76	21	87	10
11 Ruppe	58	30	50	26
12 O'Hara	31	57	39	50
13 Diggs	24	59	22	33
14 Nedzi	34	62	41	55
15 Ford	28	66	33	51
16 Dingell	21	60	46	47
17 Griffiths	34	46	45	28
18 Huber	68	24	—	—
19 Broomfield	65	29	65	20
MINNESOTA				
1 Quie	68	28	78	21
2 Nelsen	73	21	84	10
3 Frenzel	58	33	61	29
4 Karth	29	68	41	53
5 Fraser	26	67	34	60
6 Zwach	46	44	62	31
7 Bergland	34	63	47	50
8 Blatnik	24	42	29	46
MISSISSIPPI				
1 Whitten	59	34	61	36
2 Bowen	58	37	—	—
3 Montgomery	60	39	65	27

	1	2	3	4
4 Cochran	65	30	—	—
5 Lott	69	29	—	—
MISSOURI				
1 Clay	26	66	16	43
2 Symington	33	60	40	49
3 Sullivan	26	64	41	38
4 Randall	32	60	61	30
5 Bolling	38	43	50	44
6 Litton	37	58	—	—
7 Taylor	60	31	—	—
8 Ichord	51	42	65	21
9 Hungate	34	62	32	54
10 Burlison	45	54	46	50
MONTANA				
1 Shoup	54	38	67	20
2 Melcher	29	58	43	44
NEBRASKA				
1 Thone	55	45	72	23
2 McCollister	71	29	77	23
3 Martin	76	16	63	19
NEVADA				
AL Towell	57	34	—	—
NEW HAMPSHIRE				
1 Wyman	66	29	81	16
2 Cleveland	64	34	79	19
NEW JERSEY				
1 Hunt	62	22	70	20
2 Sandman	44	27	78	16
3 Howard	20	71	34	55
4 Thompson	23	56	31	53
5 Freling- huysen	70	18	78	5
6 Forsythe	62	35	70	23
7 Widnall	57	37	70	16
8 Roe	31	64	48	48
9 Helstoski	27	72	36	51
10 Rodino	28	70	41	49
11 Minish	30	66	46	50
12 Rinaldo	48	51	—	—
13 Maraziti	61	34	—	—
14 Daniels	30	62	52	41
15 Patten	32	66	52	45
NEW MEXICO				
1 Lujan	56	35	54	15
2 Runnels	36	50	32	32
NEW YORK				
1 Pike	42	57	52	48
2 Grover	60	31	79	16
3 Roncallo	59	35	—	—
4 Lent	61	28	76	16
5 Wydler	68	24	71	19
6 Wolff	37	59	38	48
7 Addabbo	31	63	40	55
8 Rosenthal	26	70	34	63
9 Delaney	32	54	61	27
10 Biaggi	24	51	44	45
11 Brasco	28	64	40	52
12 Chisholm	23	64	26	56
13 Podell	25	63	39	52
14 Rooney	4	13	51	26
15 Carey	30	54	37	50
16 Holtzman	29	70	—	—
17 Murphy	36	54	56	17
18 Koch	30	62	38	52
19 Rangel	27	65	30	56
20 Abzug	30	69	33	46
21 Badillo	14	46	29	63
22 Bingham	33	66	36	61
23 Peyser	42	43	73	19
24 Reid	18	54	43	46
25 Fish	49	41	71	19
26 Gilman	49	47	—	—
27 Robison	66	29	67	28
28 Stratton	52	38	71	21
29 King	36	10	74*	17*
30 McEwen	67	20	71	15
31 Mitchell	52	34	—	—
32 Hanley	38	58	61	35
33 Walsh	51	37	—	—
34 Horton	63	36	66	24
35 Conable	86	11	85	9
36 Smith	68	26	80	11
37 Dulski	34	57	44	49

	1	2	3	4
38 Kemp	61	29	79	17
39 Hastings	66	27	74	13
NORTH CAROLINA				
1 Jones	52	42	60	35
2 Fountain	47	50	77	21
3 Henderson	43	54	67	30
4 Andrews	42	51	—	—
5 Mizell	70	26	81	16
6 Preyer	49	50	64	34
7 Rose	41	55	—	—
8 Ruth	73	25	78	21
9 Martin	73	25	—	—
10 Broyhill	66	30	76	18
11 Taylor	50	48	65	26
NORTH DAKOTA				
AL Andrews	46	46	68	23
OHIO				
1 Keating	66	22	86	12
2 Clancy	69	25	71	22
3 Whalen	41	55	52	45
4 Guyer	58	34	—	—
5 Latta	72	28	72	23
6 Harsha	57	38	71	22
7 Brown	62	17	82	9
8 Powell	64	24	70	19
9 Ashley	33	50	50	34
10 Miller	54	46	69	31
11 Stanton	71	29	74	16
12 Devine	79	18	69	18
13 Mosher	50	42	50	41
14 Seiberling	25	73	32	60
15 Wylie	75	22	73	20
16 Regula	64	30	—	—
17 Ashbrook	50	23	52	34
18 Hays	34	50	49	44
19 Carney	28	65	46	41
20 Stanton	25	71	47	46
21 Stokes	19	48	26	53
22 Vanik	31	69	41	57
23 Minshall	54†	20†	63	17
OKLAHOMA				
1 Jones	45	48	—	—
2 McSpadden	39	42	—	—
3 Albert[7]				
4 Steed	48	46	60	32
5 Jarman	72	21	63	20
6 Camp	57	22	66	28
OREGON				
1 Wyatt	49	36	69	15
2 Ullman	38	56	46	44
3 Green	36	32	38	39
4 Dellenback	64	34	76	23
PENNSYLVANIA				
1 Barrett	30	58	37	43
2 Nix	23	63	41	53
3 Green	26	67	36	51
4 Eilberg	28	62	39	54
5 Ware	77†	21†	90	8
6 Yatron	25	67	33	53
7 Williams	66	30	84	15
8 Biester	43	52	62	37
9 Shuster	66	34	—	—
10 McDade	40	54	63	28
11 Flood	38	57	69	28
12 Saylor[8]	50†	40†	53	28
13 Coughlin	58	39	64	31
14 Moorhead	24	64	40	49
15 Rooney	27	63	50	46
16 Eshleman	66	30	66	15
17 Schneebeli	76†	20†	67	20
18 Heinz	51	45	60*	36*
19 Goodling	77†	23†	69	27
20 Gaydos	26	72	41	52
21 Dent	19	64	21	40
22 Morgan	26	53	65	26
23 Johnson	72	22	72	13
24 Vigorito	30	63	60	36
25 Clark	26	52	45	19
RHODE ISLAND				
1 St Germain	26	62	44	49
2 Tiernan	22	67	40	47
SOUTH CAROLINA				
1 Davis	41	54	48*	27*

	1	2	3	4
2 Spence	68	30	68	26
3 Dorn	55	34	62	26
4 Mann	59	34	68	22
5 Gettys	55	38	54	27
6 Young	67	22	—	—
SOUTH DAKOTA				
1 Denholm	37	54	20	61
2 Abdnor	61	30	—	—
TENNESSEE				
1 Quillen	69	24	72	16
2 Duncan	66	34	71	29
3 Baker	64	30	62	19
4 Evins	30	57	39	22
5 Fulton	30	61	34	45
6 Beard	63	29	—	—
7 Jones	42	44	48	27
8 Kuykendall	70	22	64	13
TEXAS				
1 Patman	26	36	50	30
2 Wilson	29	58	—	—
3 Collins	77	22	68	28
4 Roberts	56	36	60	26
5 Steelman	58	37	—	—
6 Teague	40	30	53	29
7 Archer	63	34	70	24
8 Eckhardt	38	58	38	55
9 Brooks	34	55	54	37
10 Pickle	50	47	57	33
11 Poage	54	42	50	34
12 Wright	39	45	63	27
13 Price	56	26	65	22
14 Young	49	47	57	34
15 de la Garza	35	54	50	41
16 White	38	54	66	30
17 Burleson	64	34	66	29
18 Jordan	30	66	—	—
19 Mahon	62	34	71	28
20 Gonzalez	26	71	55	44
21 Fisher	32	19	63	26
22 Casey	58	42	67	29
23 Kazen	40	57	59	39
24 Milford	56	34	—	—
UTAH				
1 McKay	42	40	60	36
2 Owens	32	61	—	—
VERMONT				
AL Mallary	66	32	84*	16*
VIRGINIA				
1 Downing	51	40	69	27
2 Whitehurst	72	26	81	18
3 Satterfield	65	30	64	32
4 Daniel, R.W.	72†	25†	—	—
5 Daniel, W.C.	66	34	69	30
6 Butler	75	23	—	—
7 Robinson	75	24	72	26
8 Parris	64†	33†	—	—
9 Wampler	69	30	73	22
10 Broyhill	70	26	65	27
WASHINGTON				
1 Pritchard	48	48	—	—
2 Meeds	30	67	46	44
3 Hansen	26	54	48	26
4 McCormack	23	60	39	40
5 Foley	37	57	59	36
6 Hicks	36	63	48	50
7 Adams	28	66	45	48
WEST VIRGINIA				
1 Mollohan	35	51	56	18
2 Staggers	33	61	55	29
3 Slack	40	58	50	45
4 Hechler	30	70	34	66
WISCONSIN				
1 Aspin	24	65	39	52
2 Kastenmeier	26	73	35	64
3 Thomson	70	28	73	20
4 Zablocki	44	56	74	26
5 Reuss	30	68	38	60
6 Steiger	70	26	76	18
7 Obey	26	70	38	60
8 Froehlich	60	38	—	—
9 Davis	74	17	72	14
WYOMING				
AL Roncalio	28	68	29	57

Democrats *Republicans*

FOUR GROUPS RATE ALL MEMBERS OF CONGRESS FOR 1973

Political pressure groups representing a wide range of interests annually review the voting records of members of Congress on selected issues. They then rate each member on the basis of the number of times he has supported the group's position.

Four major pressure groups are included in Congressional Quarterly's compilation of ratings for the first session of the 93rd Congress. Although the groups differ in ideology, none is affiliated with a political party. The groups are Americans for Democratic Action (ADA), the AFL-CIO Committee on Political Education (COPE), the National Farmers Union (NFU) and the Americans for Constitutional Action (ACA).

ADA ratings are based on the number of times a member voted for the ADA position on selected issues. In the Senate, live pairs (defined by ADA as occurring when a senator is present and withdraws his vote in order to be part of a pair) are included in the score. The member's percentage of support is his "liberal quotient." Failure to vote lowers a member's percentage.

Prior to 1972, ADA ratings were based upon the number of times a member voted, was paired for or announced for the ADA position. Since except for live pairs in the Senate only actual votes are now included, ADA scores in the last two years have been generally lower than before 1972.

Scores of the other three groups are unaffected by failure to vote. Thus a member can receive a 100 per cent rating from COPE, NFU or ACA if he voted on only one of the selected issues, provided he voted in agreement with the group on that one vote.

Americans for Democratic Action

The ADA was founded in 1947 by a group of Democrats "to map a campaign for restoring the influence of liberalism in the national and international policies of the United States." Among its founders were economist Leon Henderson; Wilson W. Wyatt, a former National Housing Agency administrator; Joseph L. Rauh Jr., a former District of Columbia Democratic chairman; the late Mrs. Franklin D. Roosevelt, and Hubert H. Humphrey, then the mayor of Minneapolis. The ADA national chairman in 1973 was Rep. Donald M. Fraser (D Minn.), who has served in Congress since 1963.

Senate

High Scorers—No senators received a score of 100 per cent from ADA. Nine Democrats received a score of 90 per cent or more. They were Muskie (Maine), Nelson (Wis.), Tunney (Calif.), Ribicoff (Conn.), Hathaway (Maine), Kennedy (Mass.), Eagleton (Mo.), Abourezk (S.D.), and Mondale (Minn.). The highest scoring Republican was Mathias (Md.), who received a score of 90 per cent.

Low Scorers—Nine Republican senators received zero ADA ratings: Fannin and Goldwater (both Ariz.),

Curtis and Hruska (both Neb.), Cotton (N.H.), Helms (N.C.), Thurmond (S.C.), Tower (Texas) and Hansen (Wyo.). One Democratic senator received a zero rating: Stennis (Miss.), who was absent for a majority of the votes.

House

High Scorers—Ten House Democrats received 100 per cent ratings from ADA. They were Burton and Edwards (both Calif.); Mitchell (Md.), Drinan and Harrington (both Mass.); Rosenthal, Abzug and Bingham (all N.Y.); Seiberling (Ohio) and Kastenmeier (Wis.). The highest scorer among Republicans was Whalen (Ohio), with a score of 84 per cent.

Low Scorers—Forty-seven representatives—four Democrats and 43 Republicans—received zero ADA ratings. The Republicans were Steiger (Ariz.); Talcott, Clawson, Hosmer, Ketchum and Wilson (all Calif.); Arends and Michel (both Ill.); Bray, Zion and Hudnut (all Ind.); Treen (La.); Mills, Bauman and Hogan (all Md.); Ford, Cederberg and Huber (all Mich.); Martin (Neb.); Towell (Nev.); King (N.Y.); Mizell and Ruth (both N.C.); Clancy, Latta, Powell and Devine (all Ohio); Camp (Okla.); Goodling and Johnson (both Pa.); Spence (S.C.); Quillen, Baker, Beard and Kuykendall (all Tenn.); Collins and Price (both Texas); Whitehurst, Daniel, Butler, Robinson and Broyhill (all Va.), and Davis (Wis.).

The Democrats were Waggonner (La.), Burleson and Fisher (both Texas) and Satterfield (Va.).

COPE

COPE (AFL-CIO Committee on Political Education) was formed in December 1955, when the AFL and CIO merged, to serve as the political education arm of organized labor. AFL-CIO President George Meany is the chairman of COPE. Lane Kirkland is the secretary-treasurer, and Alexander E. Barkan is national director.

COPE lists the distribution of voting records of senators and representatives as one of its educational activities, which are financed by the AFL-CIO and individual unions with funds chiefly from union members dues.

Pressure Groups on Impeachment

The AFL-CIO, Nov. 8, 1973, mailed to its members a pamphlet listing 19 alleged impeachable charges against the President. However, George Meany, March 3, 1974, said there was no longer an on-going impeachment effort.

The ADA, Nov. 20, 1973, sent members of Congress a list of 73 alleged impeachable charges against the President.

The NFU passed a resolution March 13th calling on Congress to reach "definite judgment immediately" on impeachment.

The ACA has not taken a position on impeachment.

Senate

High Scorers—Five senators—four Democrats and one Republican received a 100 per cent rating from COPE. The Democrats were Pastore and Pell (both R.I.); and Jackson and Magnuson (both Wash.). The Republican was Schweiker (Pa.).

Low Scorers—One senator received a zero rating from COPE. He was Byrd (Independent-Va.). In addition, four Republicans received scores of 10 per cent or less. They were Dominick (Colo.), Roth (Del.), Curtis (Neb.) and Bartlett (Okla.).

House

High Scorers—Eighty-three representatives—all Democrats—received 100 per cent ratings from COPE. They were Moss, Burton, Stark and Edwards (all Calif.); Cotter and Grasso (both Conn.); Pepper (Fla.); Young (Ga.); Metcalfe, Kluczynski, Collins, Rostenkowski, Yates, Annunzio and Price (all Ill.); Madden and Brademas (both Ind.); Perkins (Ky.); Kyros (Maine); Sarbanes (Md.); Boland, Donohue, Macdonald, Moakley, Burke, Studds (all Mass.); Conyers, Ford, Dingell (all Mich.); Clay and Sullivan (both Mo.); Howard, Thompson, Roe, Helstoski, Rodino, Daniels, Minish and Patten (all N.J.); Addabbo, Rosenthal, Delaney, Biaggi, Brasco, Chisholm, Podell, Carey, Holtzman, Murphy, Rangel, Abzug, Badillo, Stratton and Dulski (all N.Y.); Seiberling, Hays, Carney, Stanton, Stokes and Vanik (all Ohio); Barrett, Nix, Green, Eilberg, Yatron, Flood, Moorhead, Gaydos, Dent, Morgan and Clark (all Pa.); St Germain and Tiernan (both R.I.); Eckhardt, Brooks and Jordan (all Texas); Owens (Utah); Adams (Wash.); Mollohan, Staggers, Slack and Hechler (all W.Va.) and Roncalio (Wyo.).

Low Scorers—Twenty-eight representatives—26 Republicans and two Democrats—received zero ratings from COPE. The Republicans were Rhodes (Ariz.), Moorhead, Ketchum, and Hosmer (all Calif.); Armstrong (Colo.); McClory, Erlenborn and Michel (all Ill.); Dennis (Ind.); Mayne (Iowa); Zwach (Minn.); McCollister and Martin (both Neb.); McEwen and Conable (both N.Y.); Ruth (N.C.); Harsha, Brown and Minshall (all Ohio); Camp (Okla.); Ware and Schneebeli (both Pa.); Quillen (Tenn.); Price (Texas); Butler (Va.) and Davis (Wis.). The two Democrats were Flynt (Ga.) and Mann (S.C.).

National Farmers Union

The National Farmers Union was founded in 1903 "to do in combination what we would be unable to do separately...to strengthen and enrich the farm family." Numbering about 250,000 farm families in 1972, the Farmers Union advocates high price supports for farmers, with rigid production controls.

National Farmers Union officers are Tony T. Dechant, president; E. W. Smith, vice president, and George Stone, chairman of the executive committee.

Senate

High Scorers—Twenty-eight senators—all Democrats—received 100 per cent ratings from NFU. They were Gravel (Alaska), Fulbright (Ark.), Cranston and Tunney (both Calif.), Church (Idaho), Stevenson (Ill.), Bayh and Hartke (both Ind.), Clark and Hughes (both Iowa), Hud-dleston (Ky.), Hathaway and Muskie (both Maine); Kennedy (Mass.), Hart (Mich.), Humphrey and Mondale (both Minn.), Mansfield and Metcalf (both Mont.), Montoya (N.M.), Burdick (N.D.), McGovern (S.D.), Moss (Utah), Jackson and Magnuson (both Wash.), Randolph (W.Va.), Nelson (Wis.) and McGee (Wyo.).

Low Scorers—No senators received zero NFU ratings. Seven Republican senators—Fannin and Goldwater (both Ariz.), Helms (N.C.), Taft (Ohio), Bennett (Utah), Scott (Va.) and Hansen (Wyo.)—received ratings of 15 per cent or less.

House

High Scorers—Sixty-three representatives—all Democrats—received 100 per cent ratings from NFU. They were Bevill and Jones (both Ala.); Alexander (Ark.); Johnson, Burton, Stark, Edwards, McFall, Holifield, Hawkins, Danielson and Brown (all Calif.); Young and Davis (both Ga.); Matsunaga (Hawaii); Metcalfe, Murphy, Kluczynski, Collins, Annunzio, Shipley, Price and Gray (all Ill.); Madden, Roush and Hamilton (all Ind.); Mezvinsky and Smith (both Iowa); Roy (Kan.); Perkins (Ky.); Boggs (La.); Donohue and O'Neill (both Mass.); Diggs and Dingell (both Mich.); Bergland and Blatnik (both Minn.); Symington and Burlison (both Mo.); Melcher (Mont.); Thompson (N.J.); Podell, Murphy, Bingham, Reid (all N.Y.); Hays (Ohio); Ullman (Ore.); Flood, Moorhead, Rooney, Dent, Morgan, and Vigorito (all Pa.); Patman and Brooks (both Texas); Meeds, Hansen and McCormack (all Wash.); Aspin, Kastenmeier, Zablocki, Reuss, and Obey (all Wis.).

Low Scorers—Two representatives—both Republicans—received zero ratings from NFU. They were Blackburn (Ga.) and Collins (Texas).

Americans for Constitutional Action

The ACA was formed in 1958 at the request of a group of conservative senators to elect more "constitutional conservatives" to Congress. President is Charles A. McManus; treasurer Edward G. Orbann.

Senate

High Scorers—Three senators—two Republicans and one Democrat—received 100 per cent ratings from ACA. The Republicans were Cotton (N.H.) and Helms (N.C.). The Democrat was Stennis (Miss.). In addition, nine other Republicans scored 90 per cent or more.

Low Scorers—Four Democrats received zero ratings from ACA. They were Muskie (Maine); Humphrey (Minn.); Williams (N.J.) and Abourezk (S.D.). In addition 17 Democrats and two Republicans received scores of 10 per cent or less.

House

High Scorers—Nine Republican representatives received 100 per cent ratings from ACA. They included Steiger and Conlan (both Ariz.); Clawson (Calif.); Derwinski and Crane (both Ill.); Treen (La.); Huber (Mich.); Powell (Ohio) and Collins (Texas).

Low Scorers—Five Democrats received zero ratings from ACA. They were Rooney, Carey and Bingham (all N.Y.); Green and Moorhead (both Pa.).

SPECIAL INTEREST GROUPS RATE REPRESENTATIVES

ADA (Americans for Democratic Action)—The percentage of the time each representative voted in accordance with the ADA position on 25 selected votes of 1973. The percentages were compiled by ADA. Failure to vote lowers the scores.

COPE (AFL-CIO Committee on Political Education)—The percentage of the time each representative voted in accordance with or was paired in favor of the COPE position on 11 selected votes of 1973. Failure to vote does not lower the scores, which were compiled by CQ.

NFU (National Farmers Union)—The percentage of the time each representative voted in accordance with, was paired for or announced for the NFU position on 20 selected votes of 1973. Failure to vote does not lower the scores, which were compiled by CQ.

ACA (Americans for Constitutional Action)—The percentage of the time each representative voted in accordance with the ACA position on 27 selected votes of 1973. Failure to vote does not lower the scores, which were compiled by ACA.

---

† Scores were compiled by Congressional Quarterly from the votes selected by the organization.
— Did not receive a rating.
1 Rep. Donald Young (R Alaska) sworn in March 14, 1973, to replace Rep. Nick Begich, deceased.
2 Rep. Charles M. Teague (R Calif.) died Jan. 1, 1974. He did not receive a COPE rating.
3 Rep. Cardiss Collins (D Ill.) sworn in June 7, 1973, to replace Rep. George W. Collins (D), deceased.
4 Rep. Corrine C. Boggs (D La.) sworn in March 27, 1973, to replace Rep. Hale Boggs (D), deceased.
5 Rep. William O. Mills (R Md.) died May 24, 1973. He received ratings of O from ADA and 33 from NFU. Rep. Robert E. Bauman (R) sworn in Sept. 5, 1973, to replace Mills.
6 Rep. Gerald R. Ford (R Mich.) resigned Dec. 6, 1973, to become Vice President.
7 Rep Carl Albert (D Okla.), as Speaker, votes at his own discretion. His only rating is from ACA.
8 Rep. John P. Saylor (R Pa.) died Oct. 28, 1973. He did not receive a COPE rating.

- KEY -

ADA— Americans for Democratic Action
COPE—AFL-CIO Committee on Political Education
NFU— National Farmers Union
ACA— Americans for Constitutional Action

	ADA	COPE†	NFU†	ACA
ALABAMA				
1 Edwards	16	9	21	84
2 Dickinson	4	9	40	96
3 Nichols	8	36	80	74
4 Bevill	24	80	100	54
5 Jones	28	90	100	33
6 Buchanan	24	11	10	77
7 Flowers	16	55	89	60
ALASKA				
AL Young 1	12	64	59	74
ARIZONA				
1 Rhodes	4	0	6	73
2 Udall	84	82	90	8
3 Steiger	0	11	32	100
4 Conlan	8	18	22	100
ARKANSAS				
1 Alexander	44	63	100	38
2 Mills	12	75	67	29
3 Hammer-schmidt	4	11	53	71
4 Thornton	48	60	95	26
CALIFORNIA				
1 Clausen	8	20	60	81
2 Johnson	56	91	100	22
3 Moss	80	100	81	9
4 Leggett	64	89	88	10
5 Burton	100	100	100	8
6 Mailliard	28	64	56	52
7 Dellums	92	91	90	11
8 Stark	92	100	100	16
9 Edwards	100	100	100	12
10 Gubser	4	9	13	68
11 Ryan	64	90	72	27
12 Talcott	0	10	28	82
13 Teague 2	12	—	11	—
14 Waldie	76	75	95	12
15 McFall	48	82	100	15
16 Sisk	56	82	89	17
17 McCloskey	76	64	78	15
18 Mathias	20	18	60	70
19 Holifield	52	91	100	14
20 Moorhead	4	0	11	96
21 Hawkins	88	91	100	14
22 Corman	76	89	85	12
23 Clawson	0	10	11	100
24 Rousselot	8	9	5	96
25 Wiggins	12	10	6	86
26 Rees	96	91	83	4
27 Goldwater	4	9	11	96
28 Bell	36	56	57	29
29 Danielson	60	88	100	5
30 Roybal	92	91	94	8
31 Wilson	80	91	89	30
32 Hosmer	0	0	6	75
33 Pettis	16	36	35	77
34 Hanna	48	88	82	11
35 Anderson	92	91	75	8
36 Ketchum	0	0	25	92
37 Burke	68	75	93	6
38 Brown	88	91	100	13
39 Hinshaw	4	9	10	92
40 Wilson	0	30	17	80
41 Van Deerlin	80	91	84	8
42 Burgener	4	10	5	92
43 Veysey	8	11	32	84
COLORADO				
1 Schroeder	96	91	95	20
2 Brotzman	28	18	35	64
3 Evans	84	73	95	8
4 Johnson	48	27	83	67
5 Armstrong	8	0	20	92

	ADA	COPE†	NFU†	ACA
CONNECTICUT				
1 Cotter	60	100	74	27
2 Steele	68	91	60	37
3 Giaimo	76	91	83	23
4 McKinney	52	82	55	40
5 Sarasin	40	55	45	48
6 Grasso	80	100	80	15
DELAWARE				
AL DuPont	52	36	45	48
FLORIDA				
1 Sikes	4	36	79	73
2 Fuqua	20	40	79	60
3 Bennett	36	45	60	70
4 Chappell	8	30	75	61
5 Gunter	44	55	78	48
6 Young	16	27	25	92
7 Gibbons	52	73	85	27
8 Haley	16	36	55	78
9 Frey	16	9	37	88
10 Bafalis	16	18	30	88
11 Rogers	48	36	50	67
12 Burke	12	30	56	87
13 Lehman	76	90	95	8
14 Pepper	56	100	63	9
15 Fascell	88	91	85	7
GEORGIA				
1 Ginn	40	64	95	56
2 Mathis	8	10	71	80
3 Brinkley	24	27	89	67
4 Blackburn	4	11	0	95
5 Young	92	100	100	4
6 Flynt	8	0	61	88
7 Davis	24	80	100	43
8 Stuckey	28	55	85	62
9 Landrum	16	20	72	73
10 Stephens	16	30	79	57
HAWAII				
1 Matsunaga	84	90	100	7
2 Mink	96	91	95	11
IDAHO				
1 Symms	8	9	15	96
2 Hansen	28	30	69	44
ILLINOIS				
1 Metcalfe	72	100	100	5
2 Murphy, M.	72	91	100	4
3 Hanrahan	12	20	22	89
4 Derwinski	12	9	16	100
5 Kluczynski	64	100	100	13
6 Collier	8	18	18	80
7 Collins 3	95	100	100	6
8 Rostenkowski	68	100	94	16
9 Yates	96	100	75	12
10 Young	16	9	25	68
11 Annunzio	72	100	100	15
12 Crane	8	18	5	100
13 McClory	36	0	30	63
14 Erlenborn	20	0	22	60
15 Arends	0	9	20	84
16 Anderson	36	27	33	46
17 O'Brien	16	27	35	68
18 Michel	0	0	15	88
19 Railsback	40	36	71	33
20 Findley	56	27	44	58
21 Madigan	16	27	42	73
22 Shipley	48	91	100	46
23 Price	72	100	100	12
24 Gray	44	89	100	6
INDIANA				
1 Madden	80	100	100	11
2 Landgrebe	12	22	6	95
3 Brademas	96	100	95	7
4 Roush	80	80	100	15
5 Hillis	16	50	60	72
6 Bray	0	9	17	83
7 Myers	4	10	47	79
8 Zion	0	9	20	85
9 Hamilton	80	73	100	4
10 Dennis	8	0	5	89
11 Hudnut	0	10	15	92
IOWA				
1 Mezvinsky	96	82	100	11
2 Culver	92	82	95	4
3 Gross	20	9	25	96
4 Smith	64	82	100	13

Democrats *Republicans*

	ADA	COPE†	NFU†	ACA
5 Scherle	4	18	65	77
6 Mayne	12	0	50	58
KANSAS				
1 Sebelius	8	9	55	67
2 Roy	68	82	100	21
3 Winn	20	27	55	68
4 Shriver	8	18	50	68
5 Skubitz	20	18	68	60
KENTUCKY				
1 Stubblefield	20	55	84	52
2 Natcher	52	82	95	26
3 Mazzoli	80	55	65	26
4 Snyder	20	27	35	85
5 Carter	16	60	88	52
6 Breckinridge	40	73	90	15
7 Perkins	60	100	100	15
LOUISIANA				
1 Hebert	4	40	63	60
2 Boggs [4]	67	91	100	10
3 Treen	0	10	16	100
4 Waggonner	0	20	65	78
5 Passman	16	60	85	54
6 Rarick	16	20	63	90
7 Breaux	28	90	90	41
8 Long, G.	40	91	89	27
MAINE				
1 Kyros	80	100	94	8
2 Cohen	52	64	55	27
MARYLAND				
1 Bauman [5]	0	33	43	86
2 Long	64	70	80	33
3 Sarbanes	92	100	95	7
4 Holt	4	27	30	93
5 Hogan	0	45	40	70
6 Byron	20	45	55	73
7 Mitchell	100	91	95	4
8 Gude	76	64	55	23
MASSACHUSETTS				
1 Conte	60	50	53	22
2 Boland	80	100	83	8
3 Donohue	84	100	83	8
4 Drinan	100	91	75	7
5 Cronin	56	82	45	38
6 Harrington	100	91	90	4
7 Macdonald	72	100	82	15
8 O'Neill	76	91	100	16
9 Moakley	88	100	95	11
10 Heckler	72	91	50	22
11 Burke	80	100	90	11
12 Studds	92	100	85	11
MICHIGAN				
1 Conyers	72	100	83	11
2 Esch	60	30	45	43
3 Brown	20	9	45	65
4 Hutchinson	4	9	25	93
5 Ford [6]	0	22	15	83
6 Chamberlain	4	9	26	72
7 Riegle	76	82	89	10
8 Harvey	12	13	33	64
9 Vander Jagt	16	18	59	46
10 Cederberg	0	9	25	78
11 Ruppe	28	20	55	46
12 O'Hara	80	80	85	12
13 Diggs	76	91	100	4
14 Nedzi	80	91	84	12
15 Ford	80	100	94	19
16 Dingell	80	100	100	12
17 Griffiths	48	80	88	20
18 Huber	0	22	20	100
19 Broomfield	20	9	25	71
MINNESOTA				
1 Quie	24	9	55	54
2 Nelsen	12	9	45	65
3 Frenzel	52	9	47	44
4 Karth	72	91	94	4
5 Fraser	96	80	95	4
6 Zwach	28	0	68	63
7 Bergland	84	82	100	4
8 Blatnik	44	75	100	6
MISSISSIPPI				
1 Whitten	12	30	80	74
2 Bowen	24	27	79	56
3 Montgomery	4	18	60	85

	ADA	COPE†	NFU†	ACA
4 Cochran	8	9	55	81
5 Lott	4	10	58	84
MISSOURI				
1 Clay	92	100	95	8
2 Symington	80	90	100	8
3 Sullivan	64	100	95	24
4 Randall	36	80	95	44
5 Bolling	52	90	95	9
6 Litton	52	73	95	32
7 Taylor	4	18	37	87
8 Ichord	8	45	60	79
9 Hungate	68	91	95	37
10 Burlison	56	82	100	38
MONTANA				
1 Shoup	20	25	56	74
2 Melcher	76	82	100	19
NEBRASKA				
1 Thone	40	9	70	63
2 McCollister	4	0	45	74
3 Martin	0	0	11	80
NEVADA				
AL Towell	0	30	35	81
NEW HAMPSHIRE				
1 Wyman	4	27	42	70
2 Cleveland	20	36	45	63
NEW JERSEY				
1 Hunt	4	22	21	79
2 Sandman	8	33	38	71
3 Howard	88	100	95	4
4 Thompson	64	100	100	5
5 Freling-huysen	20	10	15	70
6 Forsythe	44	55	40	37
7 Widnall	24	55	50	50
8 Roe	68	100	75	22
9 Helstoski	88	100	85	11
10 Rodino	92	100	90	8
11 Minish	84	100	72	22
12 Rinaldo	48	91	47	44
13 Maraziti	16	73	44	65
14 Daniels	80	100	90	19
15 Patten	80	100	95	12
NEW MEXICO				
1 Lujan	20	30	44	76
2 Runnels	32	56	94	50
NEW YORK				
1 Pike	68	82	58	35
2 Grover	8	27	35	76
3 Roncallo	16	30	26	64
4 Lent	8	22	25	68
5 Wydler	16	36	33	58
6 Wolff	80	91	60	22
7 Addabbo	80	100	94	20
8 Rosenthal	100	100	85	12
9 Delaney	44	100	89	38
10 Biaggi	48	100	92	25
11 Brasco	80	100	94	13
12 Chisholm	92	100	95	11
13 Podell	72	100	100	5
14 Rooney	12	86	86	0
15 Carey	72	100	75	0
16 Holtzman	96	100	95	11
17 Murphy	48	100	100	17
18 Koch	96	91	82	13
19 Rangel	92	100	90	8
20 Abzug	100	100	90	7
21 Badillo	72	100	93	13
22 Bingham	100	91	100	8
23 Peyser	40	82	55	35
24 Reid	84	90	100	4
25 Fish	44	50	55	29
26 Gilman	48	73	60	44
27 Robison	44	9	18	54
28 Stratton	36	100	59	31
29 King	0	18	29	83
30 McEwen	8	0	31	67
31 Mitchell	12	36	61	75
32 Hanley	60	80	84	17
33 Walsh	16	67	55	50
34 Horton	44	64	55	36
35 Conable	20	0	15	63
36 Smith	28	22	22	65
37 Dulski	60	100	75	14

	ADA	COPE†	NFU†	ACA
38 Kemp	12	33	17	80
39 Hastings	16	27	41	59
NORTH CAROLINA				
1 Jones	16	30	75	73
2 Fountain	20	18	78	74
3 Henderson	24	40	90	60
4 Andrews	48	45	89	50
5 Mizell	0	9	35	88
6 Preyer	52	55	90	37
7 Rose	44	40	90	38
8 Ruth	0	0	40	85
9 Martin	12	9	40	88
10 Broyhill	8	18	67	82
11 Taylor	20	36	90	58
NORTH DAKOTA				
AL Andrews	28	45	95	41
OHIO				
1 Keating	12	9	20	67
2 Clancy	0	9	15	96
3 Whalen	84	73	60	11
4 Guyer	12	20	53	72
5 Latta	0	9	55	85
6 Harsha	16	0	63	71
7 Brown	8	0	22	71
8 Powell	0	9	15	100
9 Ashley	92	80	89	9
10 Miller	28	9	50	85
11 Stanton	28	27	32	63
12 Devine	0	9	15	92
13 Mosher	80	45	65	23
14 Seiberling	100	100	90	7
15 Wylie	24	27	21	74
16 Regula	28	18	30	68
17 Ashbrook	12	20	16	95
18 Hays	48	100	100	28
19 Carney	76	100	95	9
20 Stanton	68	100	95	12
21 Stokes	68	100	93	10
22 Vanik	92	100	75	11
23 Minshall	8	0	19	88
OKLAHOMA				
1 Jones	28	55	65	54
2 McSpadden	24	60	89	36
3 Albert [7]	—	—	—	31
4 Steed	32	82	88	46
5 Jarman	4	18	72	76
6 Camp	0	0	35	70
OREGON				
1 Wyatt	28	44	53	50
2 Ullman	52	70	100	23
3 Green	24	33	72	52
4 Dellenback	64	18	47	44
PENNSYLVANIA				
1 Barrett	76	100	94	8
2 Nix	84	100	88	5
3 Green	84	100	90	0
4 Eilberg	80	100	95	12
5 Ware	8	0	11	73
6 Yatron	76	100	94	19
7 Williams	12	36	25	65
8 Biester	64	80	60	19
9 Shuster	4	9	40	85
10 McDade	48	82	70	22
11 Flood	56	100	100	15
12 Saylor [8]	17	—	61	—
13 Coughlin	36	27	47	48
14 Moorhead	84	100	100	9
15 Rooney	60	91	100	13
16 Eshleman	16	18	39	62
17 Schneebeli	8	0	5	72
18 Heinz	60	56	50	30
19 Goodling	0	18	15	93
20 Gaydos	80	100	85	26
21 Dent	60	100	100	22
22 Morgan	60	100	100	13
23 Johnson	0	9	28	69
24 Vigorito	72	90	100	16
25 Clark	40	100	83	30
RHODE ISLAND				
1 St Germain	80	100	80	8
2 Tiernan	80	100	84	12
SOUTH CAROLINA				
1 Davis	28	80	94	50

	ADA	COPE†	NFU†	ACA
2 Spence	0	18	45	85
3 Dorn	8	45	60	71
4 Mann	24	0	63	67
5 Gettys	12	30	71	70
6 Young	4	11	35	85
SOUTH DAKOTA				
1 Denholm	68	82	95	33
2 Abdnor	4	11	75	76
TENNESSEE				
1 Quillen	0	0	37	75
2 Duncan	12	18	55	85
3 Baker	0	10	39	93
4 Evins	36	78	95	19
5 Fulton	60	91	95	28
6 Beard	0	10	50	89
7 Jones	24	56	89	48
8 Kuykendall	0	9	32	78
TEXAS				
1 Patman	24	89	100	21
2 Wilson	48	91	94	32
3 Collins	0	9	0	100
4 Roberts	12	33	68	67
5 Steelman	32	10	22	72
6 Teague	20	44	71	61
7 Archer	8	9	5	96
8 Eckhardt	92	100	89	8
9 Brooks	48	100	100	25
10 Pickle	48	45	85	42
11 Poage	20	36	60	58
12 Wright	40	80	94	24
13 Price	0	0	56	90
14 Young	28	80	85	41
15 de la Garza	24	60	84	54
16 White	28	36	85	52
17 Burleson	0	9	58	80
18 Jordan	92	100	95	4
19 Mahon	8	20	68	61
20 Gonzalez	60	91	95	19
21 Fisher	0	17	60	53
22 Casey	12	36	80	62
23 Kazen	28	64	85	44
24 Milford	16	36	50	67
UTAH				
1 McKay	44	70	94	20
2 Owens	76	100	94	26
VERMONT				
AL Mallary	44	10	40	46
VIRGINIA				
1 Downing	8	22	80	76
2 Whitehurst	0	18	25	88
3 Satterfield	0	18	26	92
4 Daniel, R.W.	0	18	30	85
5 Daniel, W.C.*	4	18	55	85
6 Butler	0	0	30	78
7 Robinson	0	9	25	85
8 Parris	5	9	25	88
9 Wampler	4	18	65	78
10 Broyhill	0	9	20	80
WASHINGTON				
1 Pritchard	68	45	42	33
2 Meeds	92	82	100	4
3 Hansen	48	90	100	17
4 McCormack	72	89	100	21
5 Foley	84	91	95	19
6 Hicks	64	91	95	30
7 Adams	92	100	79	21
WEST VIRGINIA				
1 Mollohan	40	100	94	24
2 Staggers	64	100	94	19
3 Slack	44	100	95	33
4 Hechler	88	100	85	22
WISCONSIN				
1 Aspin	88	90	100	12
2 Kastenmeier	100	82	100	20
3 Thomson	20	18	60	48
4 Zablocki	56	82	100	22
5 Reuss	88	91	100	8
6 Steiger	32	9	35	60
7 Obey	96	70	100	19
8 Froehlich	16	18	55	89
9 Davis	0	0	12	83
WYOMING				
AL Roncalio	72	100	95	27

Democrats *Republicans*

	ADA	COPE†	NFU†	ACA			ADA	COPE†	NFU†	ACA			ADA	COPE†	NFU†	ACA
ALABAMA						**IOWA**						**NEW HAMPSHIRE**				
Allen	5	36	50	70		Clark	80	82	100	4		McIntyre	65	91	88	7
Sparkman	10	70	71	46		Hughes	80	75	100	8		*Cotton*	0	13	20	100
ALASKA						**KANSAS**						**NEW JERSEY**				
Gravel	65	86	100	10		*Dole*	10	27	56	82		Williams	80	91	94	0
Stevens	15	60	64	57		*Pearson*	45	67	88	24		*Case*	85	82	75	3
ARIZONA						**KENTUCKY**						**NEW MEXICO**				
Fannin	0	20	6	96		Huddleston	55	82	100	15		Montoya	40	91	100	24
Goldwater	0	29	9	90		*Cook*	30	55	88	48		*Domenici*	10	18	38	89
ARKANSAS						**LOUISIANA**						**NEW YORK**				
Fulbright	55	67	100	23		Johnston	35	50	75	54		*Buckley**	15	11	20	96
McClellan	15	27	50	78		Long	35	82	67	41		*Javits*	55	78	94	8
CALIFORNIA						**MAINE**						**NORTH CAROLINA**				
Cranston	85	90	100	8		Hathaway	90	73	100	4		Ervin	10	27	40	67
Tunney	90	82	100	4		Muskie	95	82	100	0		*Helms*	0	18	12	100
COLORADO						**MARYLAND**						**NORTH DAKOTA**				
Haskell	85	90	93	12		*Beall*	25	45	56	59		Burdick	80	82	100	11
Dominick	10	9	33	78		*Mathias*	90	60	75	4		*Young*	5	45	53	52
CONNECTICUT						**MASSACHUSETTS**						**OHIO**				
Ribicoff	90	91	82	14		Kennedy	90	91	100	4		*Saxbe*	20	25	31	57
Weicker	55	50	47	50		*Brooke*	70	89	94	8		*Taft*	25	38	15	60
DELAWARE						**MICHIGAN**						**OKLAHOMA**				
Biden	80	80	93	8		Hart	85	89	100	4		*Bartlett*	15	9	25	96
Roth	40	9	29	83		*Griffin*	10	18	38	88		*Bellmon*	15	27	40	61
FLORIDA						**MINNESOTA**						**OREGON**				
Chiles	60	73	88	38		Humphrey	85	90	100	0		*Hatfield*	80	33	76	30
Gurney	15	30	53	82		Mondale	95	90	100	4		*Packwood*	50	20	56	36
GEORGIA						**MISSISSIPPI**						**PENNSYLVANIA**				
Nunn	30	40	63	66		Eastland	5	38	50	70		*Schweiker*	75	100	94	17
Talmadge	15	45	56	70		Stennis	0	25	71	100		*Scott*	25	55	38	61
HAWAII						**MISSOURI**						**RHODE ISLAND**				
Inouye	70	91	93	15		Eagleton	90	80	94	8		Pastore	75	100	94	15
Fong	15	36	56	58		Symington	75	67	94	12		Pell	80	100	94	7
IDAHO						**MONTANA**						**SOUTH CAROLINA**				
Church	70	78	100	22		Mansfield	85	80	100	7		Hollings	45	60	88	44
McClure	25	20	40	92		Metcalf	70	82	100	34		*Thurmond*	0	18	35	89
ILLINOIS						**NEBRASKA**						**SOUTH DAKOTA**				
Stevenson	85	82	100	7		*Curtis*	0	10	24	96		Abourezk	90	89	94	0
Percy	60	75	69	17		*Hruska*	0	18	24	93		McGovern	80	80	100	4
INDIANA						**NEVADA**						**TENNESSEE**				
Bayh	85	91	100	4		Bible	55	82	88	33		*Baker*	10	22	53	73
Hartke	55	91	100	4		Cannon	35	82	94	27		*Brock*	20	30	31	86

- KEY -

ADA— Americans for Democratic Action

COPE—AFL-CIO Committee on Political Education

NFU— National Farmers Union

ACA— Americans for Constitutional Action

	ADA	COPE†	NFU†	ACA
TEXAS				
Bentsen	55	64	71	41
Tower	0	18	29	92
UTAH				
Moss	80	91	100	14
Bennett	5	22	13	86
VERMONT				
Aiken	40	73	75	38
Stafford	60	73	67	19
VIRGINIA				
Byrd, Jr.**	15	0	29	86
Scott	10	22	13	96
WASHINGTON				
Jackson	55	100	100	21
Magnuson	65	100	100	13
WEST VIRGINIA				
Byrd	60	91	94	38
Randolph	60	90	100	29
WISCONSIN				
Nelson	95	82	100	4
Proxmire	85	82	82	28
WYOMING				
McGee	25	89	100	15
Hansen	0	18	7	96

Democrats   *Republicans*   *Buckley elected as Conservative*   **Byrd elected as independent*

†*Scores were compiled by Congressional Quarterly from the votes selected by the organization.*

HOW SPECIAL INTEREST GROUPS RATE SENATORS

ADA (Americans for Democratic Action)—The percentage of the time each senator voted in accordance with or entered a live pair for the ADA position on 20 selected votes from 1973. The percentages were compiled by ADA. Failure to vote lowers the scores.

COPE (AFL-CIO Committee on Political Education)—The percentage of the time each senator voted in accordance with or was paired in favor of the COPE position on 11 selected votes of 1973. Failure to vote does not lower the scores which were compiled by CQ.

NFU (National Farmers Union)—The percentage of the time each senator voted in accordance with, was paired for or announced for the NFU position on 17 selected votes of 1973. Failure to vote does not lower the scores, which were compiled by CQ.

ACA (Americans for Constitutional Action)—The percentage of the time each senator voted in accordance with the ACA position on 29 selected votes of 1973. Failure to vote does not lower the scores, which were compiled by ACA.

IMPEACHMENT ARTICLES AGAINST ANDREW JOHNSON, 1868

First Nine Articles

March 2, 1868

IN THE HOUSE OF REPRESENTATIVES, UNITED STATES,
March 2, 1868

ARTICLES EXHIBITED BY THE HOUSE OF REPRESENTA-
TIVES OF THE UNITED STATES, IN THE NAME OF
THEMSELVES AND ALL THE PEOPLE OF THE UNITED
STATES, AGAINST ANDREW JOHNSON, PRESIDENT OF
THE UNITED STATES, IN MAINTENANCE AND
SUPPORT OF THEIR IMPEACHMENT AGAINST HIM
FOR HIGH CRIMES AND MISDEMEANORS IN OFFICE.

ARTICLE I

That said Andrew Johnson, President of the United States,
on the 21st day of February, A.D. 1868, at Washington, in the
District of Columbia, unmindful of the high duties of his office,
of his oath of office, and of the requirement of the Constitution
that he should take care that the laws be faithfully executed,
did unlawfully and in violation of the Constitution and laws of
the United States issue an order in writing for the removal of
Edwin M. Stanton from the office of Secretary for the Department of War, said Edwin M. Stanton having been theretofore
duly appointed and commissioned, by and with the advice
and consent of the Senate of the United States, as such Secretary; and said Andrew Johnson, President of the United States,
on the 12th day of August, A.D. 1867, and during the recess of
said Senate, having suspended by his order Edwin M. Stanton
from said office, and within twenty days after the first day of the
next meeting of said Senate—that is to say, on the 12th day of
December, in the year last aforesaid—having reported to said
Senate such suspension, with the evidence and reasons for his
action in the case and the name of the person designated to perform the duties of such office temporarily until the next meeting
of the Senate; and said Senate thereafterwards, on the 13th
day of January, A.D. 1868, having duly considered the evidence
and reasons reported by said Andrew Johnson for said suspension, and having refused to concur in said suspension, whereby
and by force of the provisions of an act entitled "An act regulating the tenure of certain civil offices," passed March 2, 1867,
said Edwin M. Stanton did forthwith resume the functions of
his office, whereof the said Andrew Johnson had then and
there due notice; and said Edwin M. Stanton, by reason
of the premises, on said 21st day of February, being lawfully entitled to hold said office of Secretary for the Department of War;
which said order for the removal of said Edwin M. Stanton is in
substance as follows; that is to say:

EXECUTIVE MANSION,
Washington, D.C., February 21, 1868.

HON. EDWIN M. STANTON,
Washington, D.C.

SIR: By virtue of the power and authority vested in me as
President by the Constitution and laws of the United States, you
are hereby removed from office as Secretary for the Department of War, and your functions as such will terminate upon the
receipt of this communication.

You will transfer to Brevet Major-General Lorenzo Thomas, Adjutant-General of the Army, who has this day been authorized and empowerd to act as Secretary of War ad interim,
all records, books, papers, and other public property now in your
custody and charge.

Respectfully, yours,

ANDREW JOHNSON.

Which order was unlawfully issued with intent then and there to
violate the act entitled "An act regulating the tenure of certain
civil offices," passed March 2, 1867, and with the further intent, contrary to the provisions of said act, in violation thereof,
and contrary to the provisions of the Constitution of the United
States, and without the advice and consent of the Senate of the
United States, the said Senate then and there being in session, to remove said Edwin M. Stanton from the office of Secretary for the Department of War, the said Edwin M. Stanton
being then and there Secretary for the Department of War, and
being then and there in the due and unlawful execution and
discharge of the duties of said office; whereby said Andrew
Johnson, President of the United States, did then and there
commit and was guilty of a high misdemeanor in office.

ARTICLE II

That on said 21st day of February, A.D. 1868, at Washington, in the District of Columbia, said Andrew Johnson, President
of the United States, unmindful of the high duties of his office,
of his oath of office, and in violation of the Constitution of the
United States, and contrary to the provisions of an act entitled "An act regulating the tenure of certain civil offices,"
passed March 2, 1867, without the advice and consent of the
Senate of the United States, said Senate then and there being
in session, and without authority of law, did with intent to violate the Constitution of the United States and the act aforesaid, issue and deliver to one Lorenzo Thomas a letter of authority in substance as follows; that is to say:

EXECUTIVE MANSION,
Washington, D.C., February 21, 1868

Brevet Major-General LORENZO THOMAS,
Adjutant-General United States Army, Washington, D.C.

SIR: The Hon. Edwin M. Stanton having been this day removed from office as Secretary for the Department of War, you
are hereby authorized and empowered to act as Secretary of
War ad interim, and will immediately enter upon the discharge
of the duties pertaining to that office.

Mr. Stanton has been instructed to transfer to you all the
records, books, papers, and other public property now in his custody and charge.

Respectfully, yours,

ANDREW JOHNSON

Then and there being no vacancy in said office of Secretary for
the Department of War; whereby said Andrew Johnson, President of the United States, did then and there commit and was
guilty of a high misdemeanor in office.

ARTICLE III

That said Andrew Johnson, President of the United States,
on the 21st day of February, A.D. 1868, at Washington, in the
District of Columbia, did commit and was guilty of a high misdemeanor in office in this, that without authority of law, while
the Senate of the United States was then and there in session, he
did appoint one Lorenzo Thomas to be Secretary for the Department of War ad interim, without the advice and consent of the
Senate, and with intent to violate the Constitution of the United
States, no vacancy having happened in said office of Secretary
for the Department of War during the recess of the Senate, and
no vacancy existing in said office at the time, and which said appointment, so made by said Andrew Johnson, of said Lorenzo
Thomas, is in substance as follows, that is to say:

EXECUTIVE MANSION,
Washington, D.C., February 21, 1868

Brevet Major-General LORENZO THOMAS,
  Adjutant-General United States Army, Washington, D.C.

SIR: The Hon. Edwin M. Stanton having been this day removed from office as Secretary for the Department of War, you are hereby authorized and empowered to act as Secretary of War ad interim, and will immediately enter upon the discharge of the duties pertaining to that office.

Mr. Stanton has been instructed to transfer to you all the records, books, papers, and other public property now in his custody and charge.

Respectfully, yours,

ANDREW JOHNSON

ARTICLE IV

That said Andrew Johnson, President of the United States, unmindful of the high duties of his office and his oath of office, in violation of the Constitution and laws of the United States, on the 21st day of February, A.D. 1868, at Washington, in the District of Columbia, did unlawfully conspire with one Lorenzo Thomas, and with other persons to the House of Representatives unknown, with intent, by intimidation and threats, unlawfully to hinder and prevent Edwin M. Stanton, then and there the Secretary for the Department of War, duly appointed under the laws of the United States, from holding said office of Secretary for the Department of War, contrary to and in violation of the Constitution of the United States and of the provisions of an act entitled "An act to define and punish certain conspiracies," approved July 31, 1861; whereby said Andrew Johnson, President of the United States, did then and there commit and was guilty of a high crime in office.

ARTICLE V

That said Andrew Johnson, President of the United States, unmindful of the high duties of his office and of his oath of office, on the 21st day of February, A.D. 1868, and on divers other days and times in said year before the 2d day of March, A.D. 1868, at Washington, in the District of Columbia, did unlawfully conspire with one Lorenzo Thomas, and with other persons to the House of Representatives unknown, to prevent and hinder the execution of an act entitled "An act regulating the tenure of certain civil offices," passed March 2, 1867, and in pursuance of said conspiracy did unlawfully attempt to prevent Edwin M. Stanton, then and there being Secretary for the Department of War, duly appointed and commissioned under the laws of the United States, from holding said office; whereby the said Andrew Johnson, President of the United States, did then and there commit and was guilty of a high misdemeanor in office.

ARTICLE VI

That said Andrew Johnson, President of the United States, unmindful of the high duties of his office and of his oath of office, on the 21st day of February, A.D. 1868, at Washington, in the District of Columbia, did unlawfully conspire with one Lorenzo Thomas by force to seize, take, and possess the property of the United States in the Department of War, and then and there in the custody and charge of Edwin M. Stanton, Secretary for said Department, contrary to the provisions of an act entitled "An act to define and punish certain conspiracies," approved July 31, 1861, and with intent to violate and disregard an act entitled "An act regulating the tenure of certain civil offices," passed March 2, 1867; whereby said Andrew Johnson, President of the United States, did then and there commit a high crime in office.

ARTICLE VII

That said Andrew Johnson, President of the United States, unmindful of the high duties of his office and of his oath of office, on the 21st day of February, A.D. 1868, at Washington, in the District of Columbia, did unlawfully conspire with one Lorenzo Thomas with intent unlawfully to seize, take, and possess the property of the United States in the Department of War, in the custody and charge of Edwin M. Stanton, Secretary for said Department, with intent to violate and disregard the act entitled "An act regulating the tenure of certain civil offices," passed March 2, 1867; whereby said Andrew Johnson, President of the United States, did then and there commit a high misdemeanor in office.

ARTICLE VIII

That said Andrew Johnson, President of the United States, unmindful of the high duties of his office and of his oath of office, with intent unlawfully to control the disbursement of the moneys appropriated for the military service and for the Department of War, on the 21st day of February, A.D. 1868, at Washington, in the District of Columbia, did unlawfully, and contrary to the provisions of an act entitled "An act regulating the tenure of certain civil offices," passed March 2, 1867, and in violation of the Constitution of the United States, and without the advice and consent of the Senate of the United States, and while the Senate was then and there in session, there being no vacancy in the office of Secretary for the Department of War, and with intent to violate and disregard the act aforesaid, then and there issue and deliver to one Lorenzo Thomas a letter of authority, in writing, in substance as follows; that is to say:

EXECUTIVE MANSION
Washington, D.C., February 21, 1868

Brevet Major-General LORENZO THOMAS,
  Adjutant-General United States Army, Washington, D.C.

SIR: The Hon. Edwin M. Stanton having been this day removed from office as Secretary for the Department of War, you are hereby authorized and empowered to act as Secretary of War ad interim, and will immediately enter upon the discharge of the duties pertaining to that office.

Mr. Stanton has been instructed to transfer to you all the records, books, papers, and other public property now in his custody and charge.

Respectfully, yours,

ANDREW JOHNSON

whereby said Andrew Johnson, President of the United States, did then and there commit and was guilty of a high misdemeanor in office.

ARTICLE IX

That said Andrew Johnson, President of the United States, on the 22d day of February, A.D. 1868, at Washington, in the District of Columbia, in disregard of the Constitution and the laws of the United States duly enacted, as Commander in Chief of the Army of the United States, did bring before himself then and there William H. Emory, a major-general by brevet in the Army of the United States, actually in command of the Department of Washington and the military forces thereof, and did then and there, as such Commander in Chief, declare to and instruct said Emory that part of a law of the United States, passed March 2, 1867, entitled "Act making appropriations for the support of the Army for the year ending June 30, 1868, and for other purposes," especially the second section thereof, which provides, among other things, that "all orders and instructions relating to military operations issued by the President or Secretary of War shall be issued through the General of the Army, and in case of his inability through the next in rank," was unconstitutional and in contravention of the commission of said Emory, and which said provision of law had been theretofore duly and legally promulgated by general order for the government and direction of the Army of the United States, as the said Andrew Johnson then and there well knew, with intent thereby to induce said Emory, in his official capacity as commander of the Department of Washington, to violate the provisions of said act and to take and receive, act upon, and obey such orders as he, the said Andrew Johnson, might make and give, and which should not be issued through the General of the Army of the United States, according to the provisions of said act, and with the further intent thereby to enable him, and said Andrew Johnson, to prevent the execution of the act entitled "An act regulating the tenure of certain civil offices," passed March 2, 1867, and to unlawfully prevent Edwin M. Stanton, then being Secretary for the Department of War, from holding said office and discharging the duties thereof; whereby said Andrew Johnson, President of the United States, did then and there commit and was guilty of a high misdemeanor in office.

And the House of Representatives, by protestation, saving to themselves the liberty of exhibiting at any time hereafter any further articles or other accusation or impeachment against the said Andrew Johnson, President of the United States, and also of replying to his answers which he shall make unto the articles herein preferred against him, and of offering proof to the same, and every part thereof, and to all and every other article, accusation, or impeachment which shall be exhibited by them, as the case shall require, do demand that the said Andrew Johnson may be put to answer the high crimes and misdemeanors in office here-in charged against him, and that such proceedings, examinations, trials, and judgments may be thereupon had and given as may be agreeable to law and justice.

SCHUYLER COLFAX,
Speaker of the House of Representatives.

EDWARD McPHERSON,
Clerk of the House of Representatives

Attest:

Tenth and Eleventh Articles

March 3, 1868

The following additional articles of impeachment were agreed to viz:

IN THE HOUSE OF REPRESENTATIVES, UNITED STATES

March 3, 1868

ARTICLE X

That said Andrew Johnson, President of the United States, unmindful of the high duties of his office and the dignity and proprieties thereof, and of the harmony and courtesies which ought to exist and be maintained between the executive and legislative branches of the Government of the United States, designing and intending to set aside the rightful authority and powers of Congress, did attempt to bring into disgrace, ridicule, hatred, contempt, and reproach the Congress of the United States and the several branches thereof, to impair and destroy the regard and respect of all the good people of the United States for the Congress and legislative power thereof (which all officers of the Government ought inviolably to preserve and

maintain) and to excite the odium and resentment of all the good people of the United States against Congress and the laws by it duly and constitutionally enacted; and, in pursuance of his said design and intent, openly and pubicly, and before divers assemblages of the citizens of the United States, convened in divers parts thereof to meet and receive said Andrew Johnson as the Chief Magistrate of the United States, did, on the 18th day of August, A.D. 1866, and on divers other days and times, as well before as afterwards, make and deliver with a loud voice certain intemperate, inflammatory, and scandalouse harangues, and did therein utter loud threats and bitter menaces, as well against Congress as the laws of the United States, duly enacted thereby, amid the cries, jeers, and laughter of the multitudes then assembled and in hearing, which are set forth in the several specifications hereinafter written, in substance and effect, that is to say:

Specification first.—In this, that at Washington, in the District of Columbia in the Executive Mansion, to a committee of citizens who called upon the President of the United States, speaking of and concerning the Congress of the United States, said Andrew Johnson, President of the United States, heretofore, to wit, on the 18th day of August, in the year of our Lord 1866, did, in a loud voice, declare in substance and effect, among other things, that is to say:

"So far as the executive department of the Government is concerned, the effort has been made to restore the Union, to heal the breach, to pour oil into the wounds which were consequent upon the struggle, and (to speak in common phrase) to prepare, as the learned and wise physician would, a plaster healing in character and coextensive with the wound. We thought, and we think, that we had partially succeeded; but as the work progresses, as reconstruction seemed to be taking place and the country was becoming reunited, we found a disturbing and marring element opposing us. In alluding to that element, I shall go no further than your convention and the distinguished gentleman who had delivered to me the report of its proceedings. I shall make no reference to it that I do not believe the time and the occasion justify.

"We have witnessed in one department of the Government every endeavor to prevent the restoration of peace, harmony, and union. We have seen hanging upon the verge of the Government, as it were, a body called, or which assumes to be, the Congress of the United States, while in fact it is a Congress of only a part of the States. We have seen this Congress pretend to be for the Union when its every step and act tended to perpetrate disunion and make a disruption of the States inevitable.*** We have seen Congress gradually encroach step by step upon constitutional rights and violate, day after day and month after month, fundamental principles of the Government. We have seen a Congress that seemed to forget that there was a limit to the sphere and scope of legislation. We have seen a Congress in a minority assume to exercise power which, allowed to be consummated, would result in despotism or monarchy itself."

Specification second.—In this, that at Cleveland, in the State of Ohio, heretofore, to wit, on the 3d day of September, in the year of our Lord 1866, before a public assemblage of citizens and others, said Andrew Johnson, President of the United States, speaking of and concerning the Congress of the United States did, in a loud voice, declare in substance and effect among other things, that is to say:

"I will tell you what I did do. I called upon your Congress that is trying to break up the Government.***

"In conclusion, beside that, Congress had taken much pains to poison their constituents against him. But what had a Congress done? Have they done anything to restore the Union of these States? No; on the contrary, they had done everything to prevent it; and because he stood now where he did when the rebellion commenced he had been denounced as a traitor. Who had run greater risks or made greater sacrifices than himself? But Congress, factious and domineering, had undertaken to poison the minds of the American people."

Specification third.—In this, that at St. Louis, in the State of Missouri, heretofore, to wit, on the 8th day of September, in the year of our Lord 1866, before a public assemblage of citizens and others, said Andrew Johnson, President of the United States, speaking of and concerning the Congress of the United States, did, in a loud voice, declare, in substance and effect, among other things, that is to say:

"Go on. Perhaps if you had a word or two on the subject of New Orleans, you might understand more about it than you do. And if you will go back—if you will go back and ascertain the cause of the riot at New Orleans, perhaps you will not be so prompt in calling out 'New Orleans.' If you will take up the riot at New Orleans and trace it back to its source or its immediate cause, you will find out who was responsible for the blood that was shed there. If you will take up the riot at New Orleans and trace it back to the Radical Congress, you will find that the riot at New Orleans was substantially planned. If you will take up the proceedings in their caucuses, you will understand that they there knew that a convention was to be called which was extinct by its power having expired; that it was said that the intention was that a new government was to be organized, and on the organization of that government the intention was to enfranchise one portion of the population, called the colored population, who had just been emancipated, and at the same time disenfranchise white men. When you design to talk about New Orleans you ought to understand what you are talking about. When you read the speeches that were made, and take up the facts on the Friday and Saturday before that convention sat, you will there find that speeches were made incendiary in their character, exciting that portion of the population, the black population, to arm themselves and prepare for the shedding of blood. You will also find that that convention did assemble in violation of law, and the intention of that convention was to supersede the reorganized authorities in the State government of Louisiana, which had been recognized by the Government of the United States; and every man engaged in that rebellion in that convention, with the intention of superseding and upturning the civil government which had been recognized by the Government of the United States, I say that he was a traitor to the Constitution of the United States, and hence you find that another rebellion was commenced having its origin in the Radical Congress.***

"So much for the New Orleans riot. And there was the cause and the origin of the blood that was shed; and every drop of blood that was shed is upon their skirts, and they are responsible for it. I could test this thing a little closer, but will not do it here tonight. But when you talk about the causes and consequences that resulted from proceedings of that kind, perhaps as I have been introduced here and you have provoked questions of this kind, though it does not provoke me, I will tell you a few wholesome things that have been done by this Radical Congress in connection with New Orleans and the extension of the elective franchise.

"I know that I have been traduced and abused. I know it has come in advance of me here, as elsewhere, that I have attempted to exercise an arbitrary power in resisting laws that were intended to be forced upon the Government; that I had abandoned the party that elected me, and that I was a traitor because I exercised the veto power in attempting and did arrest for a time a bill that was called a 'Freedman's Bureau' bill; yes, that I was a traitor. And I have been traduced, I have been slandered, I have been maligned, I have been called Judas Iscariot, and all that. Now, my countrymen here tonight, it is very easy to indulge in epithets; it is easy to call a man a Judas and cry out traitor; but when he is called upon to give arguments and facts he is very easy to indulge in epithets; it is easy to call a man a Judas and he was one of the twelve apostles. Oh yes, the twelve apostles had a Christ. The twelve apostles had a Christ, and he never could have had a Judas unless he had had twelve apostles. If I have played the Judas, who has been my Christ that I have played the Judas with? Was it Thad. Stevens? Was it Wendell Philips? Was it Charles Sumner? These are the men that stop and compare themselves with the Saviour;

and everybody that differs with them in opinion, and to try and stay and arrest the diabolical and nefarious policy, is to be denounced as a Judas.***

"Well, let me say to you, if you will stand by me in this action; if you will stand by me in trying to give the people a fair chance, soldiers and citizens, to participate in these offices, God being willing, I will kick them out, I will kick them out just as fast as I can.

"Let me say to you, in concluding that what I have said I intended to say. I was not provoked into this, and I care not for their menaces, the taunts, and the jeers, I care not for threats, I do not intend to be bullied by my enemies nor overawed by my friends. But, God willing, with your help I will veto their measures whenever any of them come to me."

Which said utterances, declarations, threats, and harangues, highly censurable in any, are peculiarly indecent and unbecoming in the Chief Magistrate of the United States, by means whereof said Andrew Johnson has brought the high office of the President of the United States into contempt, ridicule, and disgrace, to the great scandal of all good citizens, whereby said Andrew Johnson, President of the United States, did commit, and was then and there guilty of, a high misdemeanor in office.

ARTICLE XI

That said Andrew Johnson, President of the United States, unmindful of the high duties of his office and of his oath of office, and in disregard of the Constitution and laws of the United States, did heretofore, to wit, on the 18th day of August, A.D. 1866, at the city of Washington, in the District of Columbia, by public speech, declare and affirm in substance that the Thirty-ninth Congress of the United States was not a Congress of the United States authorized by the Constitution to exercise legislative power under the same, but, on the contrary, was a Congress of only part of the States; thereby denying and intending to deny that the legislation of said Congress was valid or obligatory upon him, the said Andrew Johnson, except in so far as he saw fit to approve the same, and also thereby denying and intending to deny the power of the said Thirty-ninth Congress to propose amendments to the Constitution of the United States; and in pursuance of said declaration the said Andrew Johnson, President of the United States, afterwards, to wit, on the 21st day of February, A.D. 1868, at the city of Washington, in the District of Columbia, did unlawfully, and in disregard of the requirement of the Constitution that he should take care that the laws be faithfully executed, attempt to prevent the execution of an act entitled "An act regulating the tenure of certain civil offices," passed March 2, 1867, by unlawfully devising and contriving, and attempting to devise and contrive, means by which he should prevent Edwin M. Stanton from forthwith resuming the functions of the office of Secretary for the Department of War, notwithstanding the refusal of the Senate to concur in the suspension theretofore made by said Andrew Johnson of said Edwin M. Stanton from said office of Secretary for the Department of War, and also by further unlawfully devising and contriving, and attempting to devise and contrive, means then and there to prevent the execution of an act entitled "An act making appropriations for the support of the Army for the fiscal year ending June 30, 1868 and for other purposes," approved March 2, 1867, and also to prevent the execution of an act entitled "An act to provide for the more efficient government of the rebel States," passed March 2, 1867, whereby the said Andrew Johnson, President of the United States, did then, to wit, on the 21st day of February, A.D. 1868, at the city of Washington, commit and was guilty of a high misdemeanor in office.

SCHUYLER COLFAX,
Speaker of the House of Representatives

EDWARD McPHERSON,
Clerk of the House of Representatives

Attest:

CONSTITUTIONAL CONVENTION DEBATE ON IMPEACHMENT

Following is an excerpt from the convention debate on the question: "Shall the Executive be Removable on Impeachments?" (From the Journal of James Madison, Records of the Federal Convention, Friday, July 20, 1787): *

Mr. Pinkney & Mr. Govr. Morris moved to strike out this part of the Resolution. Mr. P. observed. he (ought not to) be impeachable whilst in office

Mr. Davie. If he be not impeachable whilst in office, he will spare no efforts or means whatever to get himself re-elected. He considered this as an essential security for the good behaviour of the Executive. [1]

Mr. Wilson concurred in the necessity of making the Executive impeachable whilst in office.

Mr. Govr. Morris. He can do no criminal act without Coadjutors who may be punished. In case he should be re-elected, that will be sufficient proof of his innocence. Besides who is to impeach? Is the impeachment to suspend his functions. If it is not the mischief will go on. If it is the impeachment will be nearly equivalent to a displacement, and will render the Executive dependent on those who are to impeach.

Col. Mason. No point is of more importance than that the right of impeachment should be continued. Shall any man be above Justice? Above all shall that man be above it, who can commit the most extensive injustice? When great crimes were committed he was for punishing the principal as well as the Coadjutors.... Shall the man who has practised corruption & by that means procured his appointment in the first instance, be suffered to escape punishment, by repeating his guilt?

Docr.-Franklin was for retaining the clause as favorable to the executive. History furnishes one example only of a first Magistrate being formally brought to public Justice. Every body cried out agst this as unconstitutional. What was the practice before this in cases where the chief Magistrate rendered himself obnoxious? Why recourse was had to assassination in wch. he was not only deprived of his life but of the opportunity of vindicating his character. It wd. be the best way therefore to provide in the Constitution for the regular punishment of the Executive when his misconduct should deserve it, and for his honorable acquittal when he should be unjustly accused.

Mr. Govr Morris admits corruption & some few other offences to be such as ought to be impeachable; but thought the cases ought to be enumerated & defined:

Mr. (Madison)—thought it indispensable that some provision should be made for defending the Community agst the incapacity, negligence or perfidy of the chief Magistrate. The limitation of the period of his service, was not a sufficient security. He might lose his capacity after his appointment. He might pervert his administration into a scheme of peculation or oppression. He might betray his trust to foreign powers. The case of the Executive Magistracy was very distinguishable, from that of the Legislative or of any other public body, holding offices of limited duration. It could not be presumed that all or even a majority of the members of an Assembly would either lose their capacity for discharging, or be bribed to betray, their trust. Besides the restraints of their personal integrity & honor, the difficulty of acting in concert for purposes of corruption was a security to the public. And if one or a few members only should be seduced, the soundness of the remaining members, would maintain the integrity and fidelity of the body. In the case of the Executive Magistracy which was to be administered by a single man, loss of capacity or corruption was more within the compass of probable events, and either of them might be fatal to the Republic.

Mr. Pinkney did not see the necessity of impeachments. He was sure they ought not to issue from the Legislature who would in that case hold them as a rod over the Executive and by that means effectually destroy his independence. His revisionary power in particular would be rendered altogether insignificant.

Mr. Gerry urged the necessity of impeachments. A good magistrate will not fear them. A bad one ought to be kept in fear of them. He hoped the maximum would never be adopted here that the chief Magistrate could do (no) wrong.

Mr. King expressed his apprehensions that an extreme caution in favor of liberty might enervate the Government we were forming. He wished the House to recur to the primitive axiom that the three great departments of Govts. should be separate & independent: that the Executive & Judiciary should be so as well as the Legislative: that the Executive should be so equally with the Judiciary. Would this be the case if the Executive should be impeachable?....

Mr. Randolph. The propriety of impeachments was a favorite principle with him; Guilt wherever found ought to be punished. The Executive will have great opportunitys of abusing his power; particularly in time of war when the military force, and in some respects the public money will be in his hands. Should no regular punishment be provided, it will be irregularly inflicted by tumults & insurrections. He is aware of the necessity of proceeding with a cautious hand, and of excluding as much as possible the influence of the Legislature from the business. He suggested for consideration an idea which had fallen (from Col Hamilton) of composing a forum out of the Judges belonging to the States: and even of requiring some preliminary inquest whether just grounds of impeachment existed.

Doctr. Franklin mentioned the case of the Prince of Orange during the late war...he could not be impeached and no regular examination took place, he remained in his office, and strengthening his own party, as the party opposed to him became formidable, he gave birth to the most violent animosities & contentions. Had he been impeachable, a regular & peaceable inquiry would have taken place and he would if guilty have been duly punished, if innocent restored to the confidence of the public.

Mr. King remarked that the case of the Statholder was not applicable. He held his place for life, and was not periodically elected. In the former case impeachments are proper to secure good behaviour. In the latter they are unnecessary; the periodical responsibility [2] to the electors [3] being an equivalent security.

Mr. Wilson observed that if the idea were to be pursued, the Senators who are to hold their places during the same term with the Executive. ought to be subject to impeachment & removal.

Mr. Pinkney apprehended that some gentlemen reasoned on a supposition that the Executive was to have powers which would not be committed to him: (He presumed) that his powers would be so circumscribed as to render impeachments unnecessary.

Mr. Govr. Morris's opinion had been changed by the arguments used in the discussion.... The executive ought therefore to be impeachable for treachery; Corrupting his electors, and incapacity were other causes of impeachment. For the latter he should be punished not as a man, but as an officer, and punished only by degradation from his office....

(It was moved & 2ded. to postpone the question of impeachments which was negatived. Mas. & S. Carolina only being ay.) [4]

On ye. Question, Shall the Executive be removeable on impeachments?

Mas. no. Ct. ay. N.J. ay. Pa. ay. Del. ay. Md. ay. Va. ay. N.C. ay. S.C. no. Geo-ay- (Ayes—8; noes—2.)

* *From the records of the Federal Convention, Friday, July 20, 1787; reprinted with permission of Yale University Press, Copyright (c) 1911, 1937, Vol. 2, Farrand,* The Records of the Federal Convention of 1787.
1 Crossed out: "To punish him when."
2 Crossed out "trial."
3 Crossed out "rendering them unnecessary."
4 Taken from Journal.

BIBLIOGRAPHY OF MATERIALS ON IMPEACHMENT

Books and Reports

Benedict, Michael L., *The Impeachment and Trial of Andrew Johnson,* New York, Norton, 1973.

Analyzes the events and votes of the impeachment and trial and rebuts the conventional theory that the movement was the work of a radical Republican minority.

Berger, Raoul, *Impeachment: The Constitutional Problem,* Harvard University Press, 1973.

Discusses impeachment under English law and the U.S. Constitution.

Brant, Irving, *Impeachment: Trials and Errors.* New York, Knopf, 1972.

The arguments supporting a narrow concept of impeachment, rather than the broader concept of "maladministration and misconduct by word or deed."

"The Case for Impeachment: 'Bribery, High Crimes and Misdemeanors,' " Americans for Democratic Action, 1424 16th St. N.W. Wash., D.C. 20036.

Lists 73 alleged charges against the President.

"Comprehensive Study on Impeachment," ADA World, January 1974. Americans for Democratic Action, 1424 16th St. N.W. Wash. D.C. 20036.

Arguments for impeachment and President Nixon's rebuttal.

Dobrovir, William A., "The Offenses of Richard M. Nixon," Wash., D.C., Public Affairs Press, 1973.

Analyzes alleged offenses committed both by President Nixon and his advisers.

Farrand, Max ed., *The Records of the Federal Convention of 1787,* New Haven, Yale University Press, 1937, 1966. Indexed.

Proceedings, letters, diaries of participants at the Constitutional Convention.

The Federalist Papers. New York, The New American Library, 1971. Indexed.

Alexander Hamilton's two articles numbered 65 and 66 are the two papers dealing primarily with impeachment.

"The Law of Presidential Impeachment," Association of the Bar of the City of New York, 42 W. 44th St. New York, 10036.

Reviews the substantive standards and procedures for impeachment.

"Why President Nixon Must be Impeached—Now," A.F.L.-C.I.O., 815 16th St. N.W. Wash., D.C. 20006.

Summarizes the ITT and dairy fund cases, and various other allegations against the President.

"Why President Nixon Should be Impeached," American Civil Liberties Union, 410 First St. S.E. Wash., D.C. 20003.

Takes the position that the President in his own statements admits the commission of high crimes and misdemeanors, particularly in his authorization of wiretaps and the organization of the plumbers.

Documents

"An Analysis of the Constitutional Standard for Presidential Impeachment," Prepared by the attorneys for the President, The White House, Wash., D.C. 20500, Tel. 202-456-1414.

Historical arguments and precedents to support the contention that the President can only be impeached for commission of a criminal offense.

"Legal Aspects of Impeachment: An Overview," Office of Legal Counsel, February 1974. Dept. of Justice, Wash., D.C. 20530.

Documents the complexities of the impeachment question as researched by the staff of the Legal Counsel. Appendices on impeachment history and precedents.

U.S. Congress, House Committee on the Judiciary. *Impeachment: Selected Materials,* October, 1973, U.S. Government Printing Office, Wash., D.C. 20402.

Includes excerpts from debates at the Constitutional Convention and the proceedings of the trial of impeachment against Andrew Johnson.

U.S. Congress, House Committee on the Judiciary, *Impeachment: Selected Materials on Procedure,* January 1974. U.S. Government Printing Office, Wash., D.C. 20402.

Contains the relevant material from Hinds' and Cannon's *Congressional Precedents* concerning impeachment procedures in the House and Senate.

U.S. Congress, House Committee on the Judiciary, *Constitutional Grounds for Presidential Impeachment,* February, 1974, U.S. Government Printing Office, Wash., D.C. 20402

Presented as guide to assist the Judiciary Committee in its inquiry on impeachment; concludes that an impeachable offense need not be a criminal act.

Articles

Bates, William, "Vagueness in the Constitution: the Impeachment Power," *Stanford Law Journal,* vol. 25, June 1973, pp. 908-926.

Benedict, Michael L., "A New Look at the Impeachment of Andrew Johnson," *Political Science Quarterly,* vol. 88, Sept. 1973, pp. 349-367.

Berger, Raoul, "Executive Privilege vs. Congressional Inquiry," *UCLA Law Review,* vol. 12, 1965, p. 104.

Berger, Raoul, "Impeachment for 'High Crimes and Misdemeanors,' " *Southern California Law Review,* vol. 44, 1971, pp. 395-460.

Berger, Raoul, "Impeachment an Instrument of Regeneration," *Harpers,* Jan. 1974, p. 14.

Bickel, Alexander, M., "The Constitutional Tangle," *New Republic,* Oct. 6, 1973, pp. 14-15.

Bishop, J. W., "The Executive's Right to Privacy: an Unresolved Constitutional Question," *Yale Law Journal,* vol. 66, 1957, p. 477.

Cole, Jeffrey, "Impeachment with Unconstitutionally Obtained Evidence: Coming to Grips with the Perjurious Defendant," *Journal of Criminal Law,* vol. 62, Mar. 1971, pp. 1-16.

Collins, P. R., "Power of Congressional Committees of Investigation to Obtain Information from the Executive Branch," *Georgia Law Journal,* vol. 39, 1951, p. 563.

Cox, Archibald, "Some Reflections on Possible Abuses of Governmental Power," *Record of the Association of the Bar of the City of New York,* vol. 28, Dec. 1973, pp. 811-827.

Dougherty, J. H., "Inherent Limitations Upon Impeachment," *Yale Law Journal,* vol. 23, 1913, pp. 60, 69.

Fenton, Paul S., "The Scope of the Impeachment Power," *Northwestern University Law Review,* vol. 65, Nov.-Dec. 1970, pp. 719-758.

"The Impeachment of Andrew Johnson," *The Annals of America,* vol. 10, 1968, pp. 126-133.

Keefe, Arthur J., "Explorations in the Wonderland of Impeachment," *American Bar Association Journal,* vol. 59, Aug. 1973, pp. 885-888.

"President and Congress: Power of the President to Refuse Congressional Demands for Information," *Stanford Law Review,* vol. I, 1949, p. 256.

Smith, Gaddis, "The American Way of Impeachment," *The New York Times Magazine,* May 27, 1973, pp. 10-11, 48-50, 52-53.

Stone, I. F., "Impeachment," *New York Review of Books.* June 28, 1973, pp. 12-19.